PARALEGAL

Praise for Paralegal

"I consistently recommend this book to my students. Barbara Bernardo inspires her readers to accept the challenges and opportunities of a paralegal career."

> —Diane Petropulos
> Attorney-Assistant Coordinator,
> Sonoma State University
> and past president, American
> Association for Paralegal Education

"Must reading for those contemplating a career move in this direction or those in the profession looking to move up."

> —Patricia Wirth
> former executive director, National
> Capital Area Paralegal Association

"A great resource for anyone who aspires to the paralegal profession . . . informative, thorough, and well researched."

> —Theresa A. Cannon
> former dean, School of Paralegal
> Studies, University of West Los
> Angeles

"Barbara Bernardo has taken the mystery out of the paralegal profession. [She] offers a wealth of much-needed insight into the world of paralegals."

> —Richard A. Kowal
> former director, Paralegal Studies
> Program, University of San Francisco

"I highly recommend Paralegal *for anyone thinking about entering this booming profession."*

> —Patricia Duran
> past president, San Francisco
> Association of Legal Assistants

THIRD EDITION

PARALEGAL

An Insider's Guide to One of Today's Fastest-Growing Careers

BARBARA BERNARDO

Peterson's

Princeton, New Jersey

To my husband, David, and my parents, Rose and John

About Peterson's

Peterson's is the country's largest educational information/communications company, providing the academic, consumer, and professional communities with books, software, and online services in support of lifelong education access and career choice. Well-known references include Peterson's annual guides to private schools, summer programs, colleges and universities, graduate and professional programs, financial aid, international study, adult learning, and career guidance. Peterson's Web site at petersons.com is the only comprehensive—and most heavily traveled—education resource on the Internet. The site carries all of Peterson's fully searchable major databases and includes financial aid sources, test-prep help, job postings, direct inquiry and application features, and specially created Virtual Campuses for every accredited academic institution and summer program in the U.S. and Canada that offers in-depth narratives, announcements, and multimedia features.

Visit Peterson's Education Center on the Internet (World Wide Web) at www.petersons.com

Copyright © 1997 by Peterson's, A Division of Thomson International, Inc.

Previous editions © 1990, 1993 by Peterson's Guides, Inc.

Library of Congress Cataloging-in-Publication Data

Bernardo, Barbara, 1952–
     Paralegal: An Insider's guide to one of Today's Fastest-Growing
          Careers / Barbara Bernardo.
     —3rd edition
     p.   cm.
     Includes index.
     ISBN 1-56079-894-7
     1. Applications for positions.   2. Job hunting.   3. Career changes.
I. Title.
HF5383.K4815   1997
650.14—DC21   97-3499
                                                                         CIP

Editorial direction by Carol Hupping   Composition by Linda Williams
Production supervision by Karen Hansen   Creative direction by Linda Huber
Proofreading by Joanne Schauffele and   Jacket and interior design by
     Valerie Vaughan   340023   Cynthia Boone
                       B523p

Printed in the United States of America

10 9 8 7 6 5 4 3 2 1

CONTENTS

PREFACE

W hen I wrote the first edition of *Paralegal* in the spring of 1989, jobs were plentiful and there seemed no end to the go-go eighties. While the paralegal profession was beginning to show early signs of maturing, it was still expanding. Many people and organizations (including law firms) were just discovering the valuable contributions that paralegals could make.

The second edition was written during another decade, and another time. It was the winter of 1992, when the legal profession and the economy in general looked bleak. We were in the middle of a deep recession, and the outlook for paralegal jobs (or any job, for that matter) was not encouraging.

The third edition of *Paralegal* tells a much different story. Since 1992, the paralegal profession has undergone both subtle and dramatic changes. I am pleased to say that it is now a more promising career than ever. The current economy is the strongest we've seen in twenty-five years, creating new employment opportunities. Not a day goes by when we don't hear how jobs are plentiful and people are more optimistic than ever about their future. This has naturally affected the legal profession, and law firms are hiring once again.

Paralegals are now very much in the mainstream. Indeed the U.S. Department of Labor's annual employment figures show that the paralegal career is one of the fastest-growing professions. Paralegal training programs are proliferating, and public recognition for the profession is growing, as evidenced, in part, by the fact that paralegals are being written into scripts for popular television series!

The twenty-first century will soon be upon us, signaling the fourth decade and the maturing of the paralegal profession. Paralegals have been around for many years, and attorneys, corporations, and other employers now have a good sense of how to make the best use of their skills and knowledge. There are more challenging and rewarding job opportunities than ever before.

However, all of this good news pales in comparison to the main message of the third edition of *Paralegal*. The single most important impact on the profession in the past few years can be summed up in just two words: *computer technology*. It has touched all of our lives, and the legal profession is no exception.

Interesting paralegal careers have emerged, thanks in part to the explosion of computers and the Internet. Computer technology is impacting all areas of paralegal employment—not only in *what* paralegals do, but also in *how* they do their jobs. In fact, computers have made a significant impact on how paralegals *find* their jobs as well, as you'll see in Chapter 7.

Paralegals are the prime users of the latest hardware, software, and computer networks found in law firms nationwide. Firms are being forced to upgrade their old computers for the latest models and the most up-to-date applications, and lawyers are being thrown into the information age, whether they like it or not. Here is where the opportunity lies for computer-literate paralegals whose skills go far beyond just knowing basic word processing.

For instance, innovative courtroom technology, like the real-time court reporting made famous by the O. J. Simpson trial, is just one example of the new generation of legal technology affecting litigation paralegals and how they work. And paralegals working in transactional areas of law are beginning to use intelligent document-drafting software called document assembly, or expert systems, to create sophisticated legal documents.

Then, of course, there's the Internet. A year ago, I was as skeptical as the next person when it came to its value. How things have changed in just twelve months! In fact, the Internet was an invaluable resource for me in preparing the present edition of this book.

Law firms have definitely jumped on the Internet bandwagon. They are putting up their own Web pages for the benefit of their clients, sometimes with the help of paralegals. And paralegals are beginning to do some of their legal research on the Internet because there's lots of free resources available there.

In my marketing position with a legal software company I often have the chance to demonstrate our software to paralegals. I always tell them that for paralegals, computer technology is where it's at. I encourage them to keep up to date, either in their current job or by using their paralegal experience to begin a new career with a computer technology company, as I did. It's apparent that when it comes to computers and computer software, the opportunities are limitless.

This is a great time to be a paralegal. The economy is robust, the impact of technology is growing every day, and the paralegal profession, while maturing, is still expanding. New challenges—and their rewards—are out there, waiting for you.

Barbara Bernardo

ACKNOWLEDGMENTS

I would like to express my sincere thanks to those individuals whose contributions, both directly and indirectly, made this book possible: Kathy Allen, Larry Ausink, Blanca Barrios, Tracy Bodovitz, Therese Cannon, Chyllene Cattie, Leanne Cazares, Julie Champion, Doris Childs, Tami Coyne, Patricia O. Curtis, Teri L. Dellinger-Schroeder, Eva DeNegri, Patricia Duran, Lucy Ebersohl, Shelley Franklin, Lu Hangley, Linda Harrington, E. Earl Hauss, Dick Hermann, Lyla Hines, Mary Hitt, Royanne Hollins, Beverlee Johnson, Karen B. Judd, Richard A. Kowall, Jill Martin, Carolyn McKown, Jolene Miller, Kim Morzak, Michelle Myers, Loretta Nesbitt, Lynn Pelletier, Diane Petropulos, Diane Remick, Susan Roe, Laurie Roselle, Linda E. Roye, Peggy Ruse, Jon Sargent, Mary Beth Schultz, Linda Sutherland, Denise Templeton, Laura Thomas, Engrid Tronsrue, Steve Wagner, Patricia A. Wirth, and Paul Zavalney. A special thanks to Paul Kollar for all his support.

I would also like to thank the following organizations for graciously providing the salary surveys and other valuable information: American Bar Association, *Legal Assistant Today* magazine, National Association of Legal Assistants, and the National Federation of Paralegal Associations.

Finally, I would like to thank Peterson's and my editor Carol Hupping, proofreaders Joanne Schauffele and Valerie Vaughan, and compositor Linda Williams for helping to pull the manuscript together for publication.

INTRODUCTION

The concept of the paraprofessional is not new. The fields of dentistry and medicine have been using paraprofessionals—dental hygienists and nurses—for years. Yet the legal profession discovered the benefits of paraprofessionals only a few decades ago. The paralegal profession is an innovative and nontraditional career path that is helping to change the practice of law.

This book is for recent high school or college graduates; people considering a new career, reentering the workforce, or contemplating law or business school; those who want to work in the legal industry without going to law school; and students who are attending paralegal training programs. (Attorneys who are contemplating using paralegals in their law practice will find it useful, too.) It will help you to decide whether a paralegal career is right for you by providing an inside, personal look at one of the fastest-growing occupations and answering the following questions:

- What is a paralegal?

- What's the difference between a paralegal and a lawyer?

- Where do paralegals work?

- What do paralegals do?

- What are the best specialty areas for today and tomorrow?

- How much do paralegals earn?

- What education, training, and skills are needed to become a paralegal?

- How do you find your first paralegal job?

- What advancement opportunities are available?

- What does the future hold for the profession?

The book also explains how and why the paralegal field evolved, the trends in the legal industry that affect the profession, the important role of computers in a paralegal career, and the critical issues that are facing paralegals today.

It's a flexible profession: it can be a career in itself, a stepping-stone to other careers, or a foundation for law or business school. It's dynamic: it's on the cutting edge of a changing industry. And it's challenging: the inroads into our legal system made by paralegals today will affect legal services well into the twenty-first century.

CHAPTER 1

Paralegal: The New Frontier

*I do not believe you can do today's job with yesterday's methods
and be in business tomorrow.*
Nelson Jackson

■

The profession of law is centuries old, and until just a few years ago
"yesterday's methods" worked just fine. Not anymore. The legal profession is undergoing dramatic changes, not the least of which is the
evolution of a new profession of nonlawyers called legal assistants or
paralegals. (The terms legal assistant and paralegal are interchangeable.)
This exciting and innovative profession is revolutionizing the practice of
law.

The paralegal field was formally recognized by the American Bar
Association in 1968. While the field has been in existence for almost
thirty years, it has only been in the last decade that it has been recognized
as a career, thanks, in part, to the U.S. Department of Labor (DOL). Upon
reviewing more than 500 occupations for its 1990 and 1995 employment
surveys, DOL projected the paralegal profession to be one of the fastest-
growing occupations of all. This status may be attributed to the increased
consumer demand for affordable legal services, the overburdened court
system, and the increased use of paralegals by attorneys.

In addition, the 1995 *Jobs Rated Almanac*, published by John Wiley
& Sons, Inc., rated paralegal fifth best in its study of the best and worst
jobs, using salary, work environment, employment outlook, job security,
stress, and physical demands as the criteria. This is up from thirteenth in
1992. Within the business and finance category, paralegal assistant was
ranked second.

Despite this publicity, some people still don't know what a paralegal
is or does. Even fewer know how and why the field has become such a

fast-growing profession. This chapter will introduce you to the profession and help clear away some of the misconceptions about it and, in so doing, will be a starting point for your evaluation of this career opportunity.

WHAT IS A PARALEGAL?

Simply put, paralegals are nonlawyers who perform legal tasks that were once done only by lawyers. The rationale for their existence is that many legal matters can be broken down into small components and tasks that can be delegated to nonlawyers working under supervision. The goal of dividing work between lawyers and paralegals makes it possible to deliver high-quality and affordable legal services to an ever-increasing number of clients.

The idea that paralegals can perform tasks done by lawyers intrigues me. Before I became a paralegal, I felt intimidated by lawyers, as most people do. I thought since lawyers charge so much money and use Latin words, what they do has to be incomprehensible to an ordinary person. But that's just not true. After my first year working as a paralegal, I began to experience a process that I call the demystification of the law. I knew I had completed the process when one day I read a 50-page legal document and understood all that it said!

Formal Definitions

What follows are three formal definitions for paralegals that have been developed over the past several years by lawyers and paralegals. Note that the significant difference between these definitions is the phrase "under the supervision of an attorney." The first two definitions include this phrase while the third does not.

Career Tip

Working under the supervision of an attorney is an important point because if paralegals are not supervised by an attorney, then they are considered to be practicing law and are in violation of unauthorized practice of law statutes. This is an issue that you should be aware of if you are considering a paralegal career, and it is one that will be discussed at length in Chapter 9.

The American Bar Association (ABA) adopted the following definition of a legal assistant in 1986:

> *A person, qualified through education, training, or work experience, who is employed or retained by a lawyer, law office, governmental agency, or other entity in a capacity or function that involves the performance, under the ultimate direction and supervision of an attorney, of specifically delegated substantive legal work, which work, for the most part, requires a sufficient knowledge of legal concepts, that, absent such assistant, the attorney would perform the task.*

Believe it or not, that's one sentence! But lawyers, as you may already know, are fond of using long sentences with many commas. This language is commonly referred to as legalese. As I said, after a year or two as a paralegal you won't be intimidated by it.

In 1994, the National Association of Legal Assistants (NALA) modified the definition of legal assistants as follows:

> *Legal assistants, also known as paralegals, are a distinguishable group of professionals who assist attorneys in the delivery of legal services. Through formal education, training, and experience, legal assistants have knowledge and expertise regarding the legal system and substantive and procedural law which qualify them to do work of a legal nature under the supervision of an attorney.*

The National Federation of Paralegal Associations (NFPA) prepared the following definition of a paralegal in 1987:

> *A person qualified through education, training, or work experience to perform substantive legal work that requires knowledge of legal concepts and is customarily, but not exclusively, performed by a lawyer. This person may be retained or employed by a lawyer, law office, governmental agency, or other entity or may be authorized by administrative, statutory or court authority to perform this work.*

Both the NFPA and the ABA agree that the titles "paralegal" and "legal assistant" are interchangeable; however, the NFPA prefers the term "paralegal." The NFPA further categorizes the paralegal practice as follows:

Traditional paralegal—works with supervision by and/or accountability to a lawyer.

Freelance/contract paralegal—works as an independent contractor with supervision by and/or accountability to a lawyer.

Independent paralegal—provides services to consumers with regard to a process in which the law is involved and for whose work no lawyer is accountable. (The implication of this career choice will be discussed further in Chapter 9.)

According to these definitions, a paralegal is an individual who, because of education, training, or work experience, performs various legal tasks that were once done by attorneys. But these definitions do not tell the whole story.

Informal Definitions

In order to adequately answer the question What is a paralegal?, the definition has to be refined to take into account the type of employer (law firm, corporation, or government agency), the size of the employer, the legal specialty area (litigation, corporate, real estate, probate, etc.), the types of cases handled, the employer's attitude toward paralegals, and the specific skills, education, and background the paralegal brings to the job. The role of every paralegal is defined by these factors.

In addition, they are important to consider when looking for a paralegal position. As you'll see from reading other chapters in this book, these factors can make the difference between a good job and a great one.

Another problem encountered when trying to define a paralegal is the term paralegal itself. For instance, a paralegal who works in the area of estate planning in a small firm has a totally different set of responsibilities from a paralegal who works in employee benefits in a corporation. While each holds the title paralegal, the duties performed are so different that it's impossible to compare the jobs or their salary levels. (Such differences in paralegal jobs are discussed at length in Chapters 3 and 4.)

HOW DO PARALEGALS AND LAWYERS DIFFER?

Another way to answer the question What is a paralegal? is to look at what paralegals can't do and at the division of labor between them and lawyers.

4

A Paralegal Profile

The following statistics are provided to give you a general profile of paralegals. Please keep in mind that they reflect national averages only.

Gender: 94% women
Race: 95% Caucasian
Average age: 38
Age range: 21 to 67
Average years of paralegal experience: 7–10
Employer: 71% work in law firms, down from 78% in 1991
Education:
    54%—bachelor's degree
    85%—paralegal studies (64% ABA approved)
Salary range: $9,600–$125,000
Average salary: $32,875, up from $29,606 in 1991

Source: 1995 *Paralegal Compensation and Benefits Report,* National Federation of Paralegal Associations, Inc.

What Paralegals Cannot Do

In a nutshell, paralegals aren't permitted to practice law. But what does that mean? Simply put, paralegals cannot give legal advice, set legal fees, or represent clients in court; these are tasks only attorneys can do. Everything else is pretty much fair game.

Strategists and Technicians

When I first became a paralegal, the paralegal coordinator asked me to prepare a job description of my duties and responsibilities. I had trouble distinguishing between what I did and what first- and second-year associate attorneys did. At times, it seemed as if we were doing the same things. A fellow paralegal who had been at the firm for several years pointed out the difference to me: The attorney knows what to do, and the paralegal knows how to do it. To put it another way, the lawyer is the strategist, and the paralegal, who implements the strategy, is the technician. In theory, at least, that's how it's supposed to work.

To illustrate this concept, let's say you start your own company. While you may know that it could be formed as a corporation, limited liability company, partnership, or sole proprietorship, you don't have the legal expertise to decide which would be best for your situation. So you enlist the services of a lawyer, who sits down with you, asks some basic questions, and decides that your company should be formed as a corporation.

The lawyer used his or her knowledge of the legal principles of corporations (learned in law school) to make this decision. The lawyer has decided what to do—and planned the strategy. A paralegal wouldn't and shouldn't make that kind of strategic decision, which is, essentially, practicing law. A paralegal who does would be engaged in the unauthorized practice of law.

Let's carry the example one step further. If your company is to be incorporated, certain paperwork must be prepared. But by whom? A sharp attorney will enlist the services of a paralegal to draft the incorporation documents. (If the attorney does it, be prepared for an unnecessarily high bill.) The paralegal, as technician, knows how to implement the attorney's strategic plan.

I can't emphasize enough that the parameters of what paralegals can and can't do are in part dictated by the attitudes of lawyers toward them. Some lawyers know how to use paralegals; others don't. This is important to keep in mind when you're looking for a job.

The Value of the Difference Between Lawyer and Paralegal

Interestingly, the roles played by the lawyer and paralegal in the preceding example underscore why paralegal services are increasingly valued by clients.

Think about it. Suppose in the incorporation case above the lawyer informs the client that it will take approximately 5 hours to prepare the documents. Say the attorney charges $200 per hour, and the hourly rate for paralegals is $50. Simple arithmetic indicates that it would be more economical for a paralegal to help draft the incorporation papers. Of course, the lawyer would still need to review the work, but that would only take an hour. If a paralegal is used, the client would pay $50/hour × 5 hours ($250) plus $200/hour × 1 hour ($200) for the attorney, for a grand total of $450. Compare that to the $1,000 that would have been charged if the lawyer had done all the work! You can see how paralegals help reduce legal fees.

But how does an attorney benefit from using a paralegal? First, rather than devote time to fairly routine legal tasks, the attorney can spend more time making strategic decisions that require the application of legal training and expertise. Second, lower fees tend to make clients happy—and satisfied customers are good for any business. Third, if lawyers can delegate routine work to paralegals, it is likely that the firm will be able to handle a greater volume of work. Fourth, firms need not put as many highly paid associate attorneys on staff to do routine legal tasks, which can mean a considerable savings in labor costs and over-head. The bottom line is that because using paralegals makes legal services more affordable, clients and law firms both gain.

Career Tip

The most basic distinction between lawyers and paralegals is that attorneys have the ultimate responsibility for all of the work done on a case. That's why they're paid more. I found this to be one of the benefits of a paralegal career. I was free to pursue other interests outside of work, and I never lost a single night's sleep worrying about a case. I'm sure the same can't be said for some of the attorneys I worked for. Of course, this doesn't mean that if you become a paralegal you should do less than your best possible work. It all boils down to how much responsibility you want out of a job and a career.

Other Legal Personnel

As a paralegal, you'll encounter other types of legal personnel—particularly if you work in a law firm. If the lawyer is the strategist and the paralegal is the technician, what are the functions of the legal secretary, law clerk, and legal administrator?

Generally speaking, the legal secretary types correspondence and legal documents, answers the telephone, maintains files, makes appointments for the attorney, keeps the attorney's calendar, files papers with the court, and maintains time sheets.

The law clerk is a law school student usually hired for the summer to perform legal research, draft legal documents, attend hearings with attorneys, and interview clients. (A paralegal's duties closely resemble those of a law clerk. The difference is that the clerk is given more substantive legal research and less "grunt" work, so to speak.)

Finally, the legal administrator is involved in administrative functions of the office, such as preparing budgets; overseeing payroll and accounting for the firm; hiring, firing, and other personnel functions; negotiating with vendors; handling matters related to the leasing of law office space; assessing equipment needs and purchasing equipment (such as computer systems); and managing the office.

EVOLUTION OF THE PROFESSION

As I said earlier, while the paralegal field is almost thirty years old, it has undergone extensive, even dynamic, changes. It has witnessed its own birth, infancy, childhood, adolescence and the growing pains that come with it, and, as it enters its third decade, early adulthood and maturity.

It should come as no surprise that the profession had its beginnings in the 1960s. It's easy to see how a concept as innovative as legal paraprofessionals had its roots in a decade whose buzzword was change. However, it's worth noting that even before this development, many legal secretaries performed tasks that are now performed by paralegals. The role of legal secretaries in the development of the profession can't be underestimated; they were the forerunners of the modern-day paralegal.

The 1960s and Early 1970s: Birth and Childhood

During the 1960s and early 1970s, our society experienced many social, demographic, technological, and economic changes that have had a lasting impact on our legal system. Some of these developments include:

- Changes in basic social attitudes toward work, sex, the status and role of women, the family unit, minorities, and equal opportunity;
- Rising expectations of fairness and justice due to changes in social attitudes toward equality;
- Changes in national demographics, including the size and age of the population, the birthrate, migration patterns, and family size and structure;
- Greater concentration of people in urban areas, leading to increased crime and urban decay;
- Increases in the number of government regulations and laws due to growing public concerns about worker safety, environmental pollution, and health care;
- Advances in technology and communications resulting in a shift from a production- to service-oriented economy; and
- Heightened consumer consciousness, leading to greater awareness of consumer rights and a consumer protection movement.

For the legal profession, these changes translated into a greater demand for legal services, an increase in the number and complexity of laws, rising expectations of justice, and an overburdened court system. The legal industry responded in various ways, most notably by creating a new professional niche within itself—the legal paraprofessional.

From legal secretary to paraprofessional. The paralegals we know today didn't just appear out of the blue in the late 1960s and early 1970s. The profession evolved gradually. In fact, before the term paralegal was even used, individuals who worked in private law firms and federal government agencies had been performing paralegal-type functions.

Eventually, as more demands were placed upon the legal system, it became clear that the lawyer/legal secretary team at many law firms could no longer handle the work load. As a result, many legal secretaries found themselves performing paralegal-type functions in addition to their secretarial tasks. For instance, it was common for a legal secretary to draft, as well as type, legal documents. As legal secretaries handled more paraprofessional tasks and fewer clerical ones, the new profession was born.

At the same time, a change in social attitude led to an increase in the number of federal programs serving the poor and elderly. Social workers employed in food stamp, public housing, Medicare, and Social Security programs began to perform more and more paralegal-type tasks as part of their jobs. Thus, by the late 1960s the federal government was already using many individuals in a paralegal capacity.

Formal recognition of the profession. The next phase in the development of the paralegal field was marked by formal recognition of its existence. This recognition came on many fronts: from the ABA, the federal government, educational institutions, and paralegals themselves.

The first step toward formal recognition occurred in 1968 when the ABA established its Special Committee on Lay Assistants for Lawyers. Its purpose was twofold: to study how lawyers could effectively use nonlawyers and to determine educational requirements and standards for paralegal education. Interestingly, the committee looked at other professions, such as medicine, dentistry, and architecture, that had been using paraprofessionals for years and concluded that the legal industry could profit from the use of paraprofessionals. As it turns out, history proved the committee right.

The committee has since changed its name to the Standing Committee on Legal Assistants and continues to work with national paralegal associations toward the development of standards for paralegal education. As you'll read in Chapter 5, some form of paralegal training— whether a paralegal certificate or an associate or a bachelor's degree in paralegal studies—is becoming increasingly important for people planning to enter the field. Many employers require that prospective paralegal employees be graduates of ABA-approved programs. (See Appendix F for further information.)

Around the time the ABA committee was created, the federal government recognized the beneficial role of legal paraprofessionals. In 1972, the National Paralegal Institute was established within the federal government's Office of Legal Services. Three years later, the institute began training paralegals and other individuals in the delivery of legal services to the poor and elderly.

Meanwhile, in 1974, President Richard M. Nixon signed into law a bill that set up the Legal Services Corporation, an organization intended to oversee a nationwide legal service program. The corporation used paralegals to help the poor and elderly in civil matters such as landlord-tenant disputes, job discrimination cases, and divorces.

Another important development toward recognition came with the emergence and growth of paralegal educational institutions. Responding to the increased need for trained paralegals, a handful of schools began to offer courses in the early 1970s that led to paralegal certification. Before these schools were established, on-the-job training and/or a promotion from legal secretary were the only ways to enter the field. Recognizing the growing popularity of paralegal training programs, in 1972 the ABA developed standards for accrediting formal education programs. Today there are more than 800 educational institutions that offer paralegal training programs. Of them, approximately 240 are ABA approved.

The last major development toward formal recognition was spearheaded by paralegals themselves: the formation of two major professional associations. In the early 1970s, they formed the National Federation of Paralegal Associations (NFPA) and the National Association of Legal Assistants (NALA) to further the development of the profession and protect and promote the interests of their memberships. (Joining a paralegal association is an excellent way to obtain information about the paralegal profession and develop useful contacts for paralegal employment.)

Mid-1970s to Mid-1980s: Adolescence

After receiving formal recognition, the profession experienced a difficult phase in its development. As with all adolescents, it experienced growing pains, confusion, self-doubt, and an identity crisis. No one really knew what to do with paralegals. Were they lawyers or secretaries, or something in between?

Since the field was relatively new, many lawyers were reluctant to delegate complex legal tasks to paralegals. As such, during this time, the work of many paralegals was often highly clerical—organizing, indexing, sorting, photocopying, and the like. Simply put, paralegals were being underutilized.

However, as lawyers learned to use them in more sophisticated ways, paralegals began to take on greater responsibilities. By the late 1980s, a pool of experienced paralegals had developed. These individuals paved the way for today's paralegals.

Late 1980s and Beyond: Young Adulthood

The awkwardness of adolescence has finally given way to a maturity that is sure to characterize the field in the next decade. Paralegals are now accepted as a fact of life in the legal profession. They are handling more sophisticated tasks as the lines between themselves and attorneys blur.

This is truly an exciting time to be considering a paralegal career. More than ever before, paralegals are taking the direction of the profession into their own hands. As Laurie Roselle, paralegal coordinator at a New York law firm, so aptly states, "My attitude is: Let me define the parameters of what I can do, not people who think they know what a paralegal is and does. I enjoy what I'm doing as a paralegal and I believe very strongly that the whole reason for the creation of the paralegal profession is to be able to deliver quality legal services at a lower cost than an attorney."

Perhaps the most striking example of the maturing of the paralegal profession began in 1989 when the California State Bar Association established a panel to study a proposal that would allow nonlawyers (called legal technicians) to provide routine legal services directly to the public. This was an unprecedented move on the part of a state bar association. Although the California state bar voted down the proposal in 1991, other states are now considering similar proposals concerning legal technicians. If even one of these states allows such a proposal to pass, it will be a turning point for the profession, since it will mean paralegals can offer services without the supervision of attorneys.

Career Tip

Despite the advances the profession has made and the encouraging signs of increased responsibilities and opportunities for paralegals in the future, you should be aware that even today there are lawyers who have yet to recognize the benefits of using paralegals. It's not unusual to find a law firm where there are some lawyers who refuse to use paralegals, who are working next door to other lawyers who can't live without them. When looking for a paralegal job, don't be surprised if you run into lawyers who still believe paralegals are nothing more than glorified clerical workers.

DEVELOPMENTS IN THE LEGAL INDUSTRY THAT AFFECT PARALEGALS

A 1994 survey by Global Research asked large law firms to name the biggest challenges they face in the years ahead. Their top three were pricing pressures, competition, and changing client attitudes toward valuing legal services. Indeed, there have been substantial changes in the legal profession in the past decade that have directly affected the paralegal field and will continue to do so, negatively and positively. They are bound to affect you in one way or another if you choose to pursue a paralegal career.

Growth of the Legal Services Industry

In recent years, there has been an unprecedented rethinking of the U.S. civil justice system. Congressional advisory committees are examining ways to overhaul the federal rules of civil procedure, cut costs, and speed up cases through the courts.

While some lawyers are questioning this reform as a threat to the cornerstones of our legal system, namely, individual rights and access to the courts, nearly everyone agrees that there is an ever-growing demand for legal services. In 1983 the U.S. Department of Labor (DOL) reported a total of 502,000 workers employed in the legal services industry. This increased to 927,000 in 1994 (the most recent DOL report to date), with a projected 1,270,000 by the year 2005. Between 1985 and 1994, the amount spent on legal services more than doubled, from $53 billion to $114 billion.

Greater demand for services has meant more lawsuits. Since 1960, the number of civil suits in federal courts has soared 300 percent, even after dropping from a peak in 1985. The legal industry responded to this increased workload by employing more workers, including paralegals.

Between 1980 and 1990, the number of paralegal jobs increased 150 percent, from 36,000 to over 90,000. This increased to 110,000 in 1994 with 175,000 estimated in the year 2005, representing a 58 percent increase in employment. (Since the U.S. Department of Labor didn't begin to gather information about those working as paralegals until 1980, it's difficult to provide accurate statistics prior to that time.) This compares to a job growth rate of 28 percent for lawyers and 12.2 percent for the general workforce.

Job Gowth, 1994-2005

Bureau of Labor Statistics estimates, in percentages

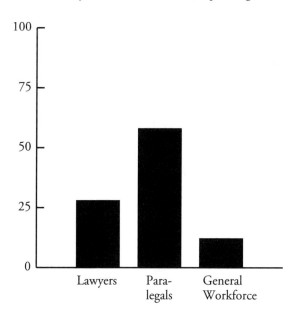

Source: Reprinted with the permission of *The National Law Journal,* copyright, 1997. The New York Law Publishing Company.

Increased Demand for Affordable Legal Services

"Affordability" is the buzzword in the legal industry today. People across the country are fed up with the high price of lawyers and are demanding high-quality services at reasonable prices. Fees have soared from an average of $20 an hour in 1960 to $150 an hour in the 1980s. Many large law firms charge as much as $350 to $400 per hour for the services of their senior partners. Consequently, virtually everyone, from the little guy to the multinational corporation, now scrutinizes legal bills. Gone are the days when a typical invoice might state, "For legal services rendered: $50,000"—no questions asked! Times have changed.

The demand for affordable legal services means that paralegals can play a pivotal role in the future delivery of those services. Lawyers can no longer ignore the benefits of using them. As I pointed out earlier, paralegals are cost effective for the client and the firm.

Oversupply of Lawyers

How many times have you heard someone complain that there are just too many lawyers? From 1970 to 1990, the number of lawyers grew more than 100 percent, from 350,000 to 750,000. According to the American Bar Association, there are currently 946,500 attorneys. To make a comparison, Japan has only 14,000 lawyers, compared to 894,000 in the United States, and the United States has only twice Japan's population!

Interestingly, unlike the U.S. legal system, the Japanese system actually discourages litigation. Japan's answer to legal reform includes: limiting the number of attorneys by passing only 2 percent of those taking the bar exam; banning discovery; forcing plaintiffs to pay an up-front fee to attorneys of up to 8 percent of damages sought; letting judges and not juries set damage awards, which rarely exceed $150,000 even if someone is killed; barring fee-sharing devices such as class action suits, which make it easier to sue; and nurturing a strong cultural attitude that confrontation is to be avoided and is looked down upon.

The proven cost effectiveness of paralegals raises the question of whether we need more lawyers or more paralegals. The answer is tricky. We actually need both. But in what proportion? The law of supply and demand would seem to be on the side of the paralegal. Today, for reasons related primarily to productivity and cost savings, a law firm is more apt to hire two experienced paralegals and one associate rather than three associates, as they might have done in the past. (That's another reason the employment outlook for paralegals is so favorable.)

Increased Competition

Interestingly, as the number of lawyers has increased, competition within the legal industry has increased as well. Adding to this pressure is the growing number of clients who shop around for the lowest possible legal fees. All of this has forced law firms to reexamine the way they do business. Firms' responses, although varied, often include the use of paralegals to help reduce client bills. (I have yet to meet a client who objects to a lower bill!)

Advertising and Marketing

Another response to increased competition is the use of advertising and marketing to attract clients. While these techniques have been used for many years by most businesses, the courts relaxed the rules governing advertising by lawyers only within the last decade. The result is that firms are beginning to make use of marketing and public relations professionals. This may be good news for paralegals who want to use their career as a stepping-stone to a job in public relations or marketing, as you will see in Chapter 8.

Greater Specialization

In recent years, there has been a trend toward greater specialization within the law. As with medicine, the days of the general practitioner are gone. There is just too much information for any one person to know. Thus, lawyers are becoming experts in specific areas of law, such as taxation, securities, bankruptcy, immigration, and so forth, and "boutique" law firms that offer expertise in a particular specialty area are emerging.

What does this mean for the paralegal? Everything! The trend toward specialization is an important key to higher salary and greater paralegal job satisfaction.

Computers and Technology

Computers are revolutionizing law offices everywhere and are changing the nature of paralegal jobs. Until just recently, law offices used computers primarily for billing purposes and word processing. Only the largest firms had the luxury to purchase litigation support systems worth tens of thousands of dollars. Not any more. Law firms of all sizes are jumping on the technology bandwagon, thanks to the increase in microprocessor speed and the decrease in the cost of personal computers.

That's not to say that all lawyers are wholeheartedly embracing technology. In fact, many of them are still resisting. The smart ones, however, have recognized that one of the ways to stay competitive is to automate their practice. Today, for example, legal computer software includes litigation support systems, case management, legal research, courtroom graphics, imaging systems, and cutting-edge technology called

Pluses and Minuses of a Paralegal Career

These are based on my own personal experience and those of other paralegals I have spoken to along the way. Keep in mind that many are purely subjective.

Benefits include:

- Challenging and interesting work with unlimited opportunity to learn
- Paralegal jobs available in a wide variety of legal practice areas
- Project-oriented assignments
- Opportunity to work with minimal supervision
- Ability to earn a good salary in comparison to years of education required
- Opportunity to become part of a new career that is changing the practice of law
- Ability to use paralegal skills and knowledge as a foundation for law school, business school, and other careers
- Opportunity to work in law without investing time and money in law school or without becoming a legal secretary
- Growing opportunities in nonlegal job areas
- Excellent career to pursue if you "want a life" outside of work or have other interests

Disadvantages include:

- New career still defining itself
- Underutilization of paralegals by some attorneys unwilling to delegate substantive assignments
- Lack of consistency in perception by employers as to whether or not paralegals are true professionals
- Difficult to earn respect from some attorneys
- Do not have ultimate responsibility
- Job responsibilities are so diverse that job satisfaction varies greatly from paralegal to paralegal
- Salaries will never match those of lawyers even though they do a lot of work lawyers used to do

expert systems. These software programs mimic how a lawyer thinks and analyzes legal problems by combining legal research with document drafting in one process.

For paralegals, the trend toward the increased use of computers and technology is a gold mine! Computer-literate paralegals tend to enjoy greater job satisfaction, increased compensation, and more avenues for career advancement, as you'll read in Chapter 6. I can't emphasize enough how important it will be in the future for paralegals to become computer literate.

Alternative Methods of Dispute Resolution

An overburdened judicial system and expensive litigation proceedings have resulted in the use of less formal methods of resolving disputes. One such method is arbitration. In it, disputing parties mutually agree to settle the matter by employing a disinterested party, known as an arbitrator, to make a decision that will be binding for them. Another is mediation. It's a less formal, nonbinding method of dispute resolution. The most familiar use of arbitrators and mediators is in the areas of labor disputes and sports negotiations. While alternative dispute resolution (ADR) methods have been slow to catch on, this is changing. The Administrative Dispute Resolution Act of 1990 requires all federal agencies to develop ADR policies.

The use of paralegals in ADR is increasing. Paralegals not only are assisting lawyers in traditional ways but also are using this experience to advance into careers as arbitrators and mediators.

Self-Help Law

Among the more controversial developments is the notion of self-help law. In 1971, Ralph Warner and Charles Sherman pioneered the self-help law movement by cofounding Nolo Press in Berkeley, California, and establishing the WAVE Project. Nolo Press publishes self-help law practice books and computer software such as *How to Do Your Own Divorce* and *How to Form Your Own Corporation*.

The WAVE Project was the country's first self-help law center where nonlawyers specialize in preparing divorce forms at significantly lower rates than those charged by attorneys. The concept that guides the movement is that the average person can use self-help publications to draft legal documents that lawyers then need only review, which helps the user save on form preparation, consulting, and other such attorney fees.

One recent innovation in self-help law is the installation of user-friendly computer kiosks in the courthouses of Maricopa County, Arizona, where individuals can get answers to a variety of legal questions as well as generate court-approved forms for filing in domestic relations proceedings.

Not surprisingly, not everyone in the legal profession is pleased with this concept. Some lawyers believe that filling out the forms needed to prepare one's own divorce or incorporation dangerously walks the line of unauthorized practice of law.

Beyond the WAVE Project, there are paralegals who, with do-it-yourself publications like those from Nolo Press, have started their own paralegal businesses and offer legal services directly to the general public. These independent paralegals have come under a great deal of criticism from the legal profession in general and from some paralegals. The concern is that they may be engaged in the unauthorized practice of law.

Responding to this criticism, the proponents of self-help law ask whether the lawyers are unselfishly concerned with protecting the general public against the unauthorized practice of law or more concerned about possible competition from nonlawyers. This controversial issue is discussed in Chapter 9.

More Effective Use of Paralegals

Over the past three decades—since the birth of the profession—there has been an increasing trend toward hiring more paralegals and using them more effectively. Paralegals are proving their worth not only in terms of the bottom line but also in their work product. Lawyers are

---

Paralegal Job Satisfaction

While job satisfaction is difficult to quantify, the NFPA's 1995 *Paralegal Compensation and Benefits Report* did just that. Based on salary, bonus, benefits, professional status, responsibility, and high workload, respondents assessed their jobs with the following results:

Overall	*Bonus*	*Professional Status*
11% very high	12% very satisfied	24% very satisfied
40% high	36% satisfied	54% satisfied
36% medium	52% dissatisfied	22% dissatisfied
10% low		
3% very low	*Benefits*	*Responsibility*
	30% very satisfied	37% very satisfied
Salary	53% satisfied	47% satisfied
13% very satisfied	17% dissatisfied	16% dissatisfied
55% satisfied		
32% dissatisfied		

---

beginning to realize that paralegals can do much more than index and organize documents and are trusting them to perform more of the tasks that they once did themselves.

A stellar example of paralegal utilization can be found at the Law Offices of Edward A. Smith, a personal injury attorney in Sacramento, California. Since beginning his practice in 1983, Mr. Smith has hired nine paralegals and no attorneys. His innovative approach is due to his belief that paralegals are capable of performing many tasks currently done by attorneys. In this case, everyone benefits: Mr. Smith, his paralegals, and his clients!

However, not all paralegals feel they are performing high-level, sophisticated work. Some are frustrated because they're being underutilized by attorneys. This is a continual issue in the profession and one that will be discussed in Chapter 9.

Downsizing

Throughout most of this century, the legal profession seemed to be immune to recessionary forces. But the economic downturn of the early 1990s hit the legal profession hard. Consolidations, mergers, and bankruptcies resulted in the unthinkable—attorney layoffs, which, in turn, negatively affected paralegal employment. Now, it looks like the dust has settled and the number of layoffs and reorganizations have leveled off. Layoffs do still happen, but most of them appear to be attorney layoffs in large firms, and these have actually created new opportunities for paralegals. Many attorneys who've left the bigger firms have opened up new small firms and sole practitioner offices, which, in turn, have hired paralegals to work with them.

Bankruptcies are now a fact of life, but they're relatively rare in the legal industry. The legal profession is still one of the more stable areas of employment. But the possibility of bankruptcy has compelled lawyers to see that they have to do more than just practice law—they need to run their law firms like businesses. And a good way to remain competitive is to effectively use paralegals.

These are the trends and developments that are shaping and defining the paralegal profession. All will have some bearing on the role and responsibilities of those who enter the field in the 1990s and later.

Now that you have a better understanding of what a paralegal is, as well as some of the advantages and disadvantages of a paralegal career, you can begin to decide whether this career is for you. Of course, you'll need information about the specific tasks and responsibilities of paralegals in order to make a full evaluation. But before you look at those, it's important to consider where paralegals work. The workplace helps determine the work environment and, to some degree, the specific duties of paralegals. The next chapter examines this matter.

CHAPTER 2

Where Do Paralegals Work?

*Nothing is really work unless you would
rather be doing something else.*
Chub De Wolfe

■

My first position in law was in 1979 in a small law firm in Hartford, Connecticut. On my second day on the job, one of the attorneys took me aside and said, "I just want you to know that lawyers are a strange breed that take some getting used to." At the time, I had no idea what he was talking about, since the only contact I had with attorneys up until then had to do with a relative's will. But now I can unequivocally say that he was right—they do take some getting used to, and so does working in a law firm!

For some people, the thought of visiting a law firm, much less working in one, can be quite intimidating. Just looking at all those law books can make them nervous! On the other hand, there are some who find the level of professionalism and intensity at a law firm quite stimulating and challenging.

But, while law firms may be the largest employer of paralegals, they certainly aren't the only employer. Others include corporations; banks; insurance companies; federal, state, and local government agencies; nonprofit corporations; legal aid organizations; and paralegal service companies. There are significant differences between working in these organizations in terms of assignments, salary, benefits, advancement possibilities, and job satisfaction.

LAW FIRMS

There are over 42,000 law firms in the United States with two or more attorneys. Since the majority of paralegals—approximately 75 percent—

work in them, that's where this discussion begins. Law firms come in all shapes and sizes and range from sole practitioners to megafirms with over 1,000 lawyers. This was not always the case. In an article that appeared in a law journal in 1902, the author made reference to "the giant law firms of five to as many as eight lawyers." How times have changed.

In the past decade, law firms have undergone many transformations. The 1980s saw law firms increase in size from an average of approximately 100 lawyers in 1978 to 200 lawyers in 1987. Also, many firms opened branch offices abroad in response to the globalization of our economy. Growth in firm size resulted in growth in revenues. In 1987, 21 of the top 100 law firms in the nation had revenues exceeding $100 million—the size of some Fortune 1000 companies! Suddenly, law became big business.

In contrast, the 1990s have been characterized by layoffs and downsizing. Law firms stopped growing as the recession hit and clients, particularly in the transactional areas of corporate and real estate, became scarce. However, as a result of these layoffs, many lawyers who used to work in large firms started their own firms, creating new opportunities for paralegals.

Who Employs Paralegals?

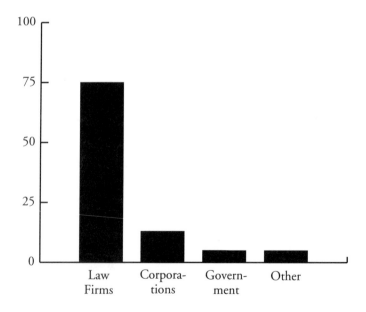

Law Firm Structure and Personnel

Basically, a firm is either a partnership or a professional corporation, with some variations (see the discussions of LLP, or limited liability partnership, and LLC, or limited liability company elsewhere in the book). What this means is that a limited number of individuals—the partners or shareholders—own the firm and share in its profits. Think of a law firm as a pyramid: the partners are at the top and are supported by a larger group of people below them.

The goal of most lawyers is to become a partner, and this is usually achieved by working for approximately seven years as an associate, which is the level on the pyramid below partner. But as competition between firms increases and profit margins are squeezed, becoming a partner is easier said than done. These days, there are no guarantees that just because an attorney has devoted seven years to a firm he or she will be made a partner.

Some associates are hired directly out of law school; others are hired from other law firms. Paralegals usually work more with associates than with partners. It's been my experience that associates fresh out of law school generally know less about how to get things done than paralegals with several years' experience. As a result, new associates are sometimes reluctant to ask paralegals for help, but must eventually come to realize that an experienced paralegal is an invaluable asset.

The rest of the pyramid consists of the support staff, including:

- Paralegals and paralegal assistants (sometimes known as case assistants);

- The law clerk;

- The administrative staff, such as librarians, personnel managers, legal administrators, information technology managers, and marketing administrators; and

- Clerical staff, such as secretaries, word processors, messengers, receptionists, and file clerks.

Some of these were discussed in more detail in Chapter 1.

As a paralegal, you'll interact with all or some of these other support staffers daily. The order of this list is not meant to imply that any one group is more important than another. (You'll find out just how important the file clerk's job is when a file has been misplaced!) And, depending on the size of the firm, some of the positions may not exist. For instance, a small law firm usually doesn't have a librarian or in-house messengers.

Career Tip

It's important to understand that the responsibilities and duties of some of the administrative staff may overlap those of paralegals, depending on the size of the law firm, the attitude of the firm toward each position, and the firm's budget. For instance, in a small law firm with a limited budget, the paralegal may be required to perform some of the functions of a legal administrator, legal secretary, or librarian.

Paralegals and legal secretaries. Paralegals generally share a secretary with a partner, one or two associates, or any combination of the two. I would be remiss if I didn't mention the tension that may exist between legal secretaries and paralegals; there are several reasons for it. The occupation of legal secretary has been around much longer than that of paralegal. Also, as I mentioned earlier, in a sense legal secretaries were the forerunners of paralegals. I've found that a lawyer generally develops a special relationship with his or her secretary: each is devoutly loyal to the other.

What does this mean for the paralegal? Basically, be good to the secretary. I know it sounds trite, but in reality a secretary can make your life infinitely easier or make it miserable. The bottom line is that the partner, associate, paralegal, and secretary must all work together to deliver the best possible service to the client.

Clients

Clients come in many shapes and sizes. They may be individuals, small companies, multinational corporations, or something in between. When I was with a large law firm, the clients I worked for included banks, brokerage firms, a multinational oil company, start-up high-tech computer companies, restaurants and wineries, an ice-cream manufacturer, a department store, a lily bulb grower, an exporter of Oriental goods, a sugar company, and a mining company.

It's important to understand that the type of work performed by paralegals in law firms is directly related to the firm's clientele. In turn, the clientele is usually determined by the size of the law firm. For instance, most individuals and small companies can't afford the expensive rates charged by large firms. As a result, the majority of the clients of large law firms are corporations. It follows then that, no matter what legal specialty area the paralegal works in, the assignments in a large law firm are likely to involve the affairs of a corporation.

Billable Hours

Common to all firms, no matter what their size, is the notion of billable and nonbillable hours. Clients are charged on an hourly basis for the services performed by the partners, associates, paralegals, and paralegal assistants, and, at times, for word processing. Generally, firms don't charge for a secretary's time.

What does this mean for you as a paralegal? It means you must account for most or all of your time each day—your billable and nonbillable hours. Billable hours are those spent on matters that can be charged directly to clients. Nonbillable hours are spent on matters that are not directly related to clients, such as administrative tasks and pro bono work. (*Pro bono publico* is Latin for "for the public good or welfare" and means a case taken on for free. These can be the most interesting cases to work on.)

Billable hours are directly related to the firm's profits. Firms usually set a minimum number of billable hours for paralegals, as they do for attorneys. With law firms becoming more cost conscious, more firms than ever before require their paralegals to bill a minimum number of hours per year—usually somewhere between 1,200 and 1,800. What these numbers mean in terms of your job search will be discussed more fully in Chapter 7.

Law Firm Size

The question now is what size law firm to work in—large, medium, or small? I've worked in all three and can honestly say that each has its pros and cons. Other than legal specialty area, the size of the firm you work in will have the greatest impact on your job. Since the downsizing of the large firms began in the early 1990s, more opportunities are opening up in newly created small firms and sole practitioners offices.

The size of a law firm is relative and depends on the number of attorneys it employs and its geographic location. For instance, a medium-size law firm in New York City may employ 200 lawyers, while a firm with the same number of attorneys in a smaller city might be considered large. For simplicity's sake, let's say that large means 100 or more lawyers, medium is fifty to ninety-nine lawyers, and small is one to forty-nine lawyers.

> ## Law Firms—Employer Summary
>
> *Characteristics:* Employ 75 percent of all paralegals; require bill-able hours; work for multiple clients.
>
> *Advantages:* Good foundation and experience; large job market; most likely employer for first job; salary and bonuses often higher than corporations.
>
> *Disadvantages:* Stressful environment due to billable-hour require-ments; overtime often required, particularly for cases involving litigation.

Large law firms. Large firms are usually organized by specialty groups—litigation, bankruptcy, real estate, probate, securities, and so on. Each group has a supervising partner, and the partner has a number of associates working under her or him. At least one paralegal is assigned to each group. As a result, the paralegals, as well as the attorneys, become specialists in the area. In small firms, paralegals often work in more than one specialty area. As you can see, the size of the firm is an important factor when considering paralegal employment.

Working in a large firm has several advantages. The most obvious is that a large firm has more resources to tap into—an extensive law library, photocopy and word processing centers, and in-house messengers, among other things. I can recall going from a small firm of fourteen attorneys in New York to a large firm of 200-plus attorneys in San Francisco. What struck me first was that in the large firm I could delegate the more routine tasks to various departments. At the small firm, if I wanted three copies of a 100-page document and the secretary was busy, guess who did it? The structure at a large firm allows paralegals to perform more sophisticated tasks and not spend valuable time at the copy machine.

A wonderful development is the advent of case assistants who help paralegals working on large cases. Case assistants do a lot of the docu-ment organization, indexing, and general clerical work. A case assistant career track in a law firm provides another opportunity for individuals to be promoted to paralegals.

A large firm may also offer a structured paralegal system that might include a paralegal manager, an in-house paralegal training program, paralegal staff meetings, in-house seminars, and in-house advancement opportunities. I found it quite beneficial to have a paralegal supervisor available to act as the liaison between management and me regarding work assignments and salary. In-house training, which includes the use of the law library and computerized legal research systems, is particularly useful to new paralegals who don't have much job experience. Large firms regularly schedule paralegal staff meetings and seminars on various legal topics, which offer the opportunity to network and get to know fellow paralegals. (The larger the firm, the more paralegals.)

Career Tip

Unfortunately, not all law firms use case assistants. As a result, some paralegals spend more of their time on clerical tasks, which can create frustration and dissatisfaction and lead to high turnover rates. Whether a firm uses case assistants is an important consideration when looking for your first paralegal job. This will be discussed further in Chapter 7.

Also, many large firms that wish to retain experienced paralegals have created a senior paralegal job track. This advanced position often includes certain perquisites such as a higher salary range, a bonus, more vacation, and paid parking. Large means greater specialization in terms of paralegal assignments. Paralegals become specialists rather than generalists, and salaries for specialists are usually higher than those for generalists.

Of course, there's a downside to working in a large law firm. As with all large organizations, it's difficult to cut through policies and procedures. In other words, it may be easier to negotiate a salary in a small firm than in a large one, where salary is tied to a stringent policy.

Large Law Firms—Employer Summary

Characteristics: Formal atmosphere; clients are generally larger corporations; opportunity to specialize.

Advantages: Greater resources, including a paralegal manager as well as an in-house training program for entry-level paralegals; opportunity to change jobs within firm; may have senior paralegal career track as well as case assistants.

Disadvantages: Greater bureaucracy when setting salaries.

Small law firms. The primary advantage of working in a small firm is the flexibility in assignments and the ambiance of the firm—the atmosphere is usually less formal and more relaxed than in large ones. The greatest disadvantage is the limited amount of resources. Most small firms generally don't have word processing or photocopying centers, in-house messengers, a paralegal coordinator/supervisor, an extensive law library, or a senior paralegal career track.

In addition, paralegals in a small firm may have to perform administrative and/or secretarial duties due to budgetary constraints. These tasks may or may not be desirable, depending on personal preferences and career plans. For instance, if you'd like to move into the area of legal administration, some experience performing administrative tasks would be helpful. Small firms can facilitate such cross-experience more easily than large ones.

Career Tip

Be wary of a job that requires you to be both secretary and paralegal. Your salary may be lower, and you'll end up performing more clerical tasks than paralegal ones.

Paralegal salaries in small firms may or may not be comparable to those in large firms. Much depends on the attitude of the firm toward paralegals. If the firm is sophisticated in its use of paralegals, the salary will reflect this. On the other hand, if a firm wants to cut costs or doesn't know how to properly utilize paralegals, it won't offer salaries comparable to those in large firms.

Career Tip

Remember that law firm size is an important consideration when looking for your first paralegal job because it will affect both your job satisfaction and your responsibilities.

Many paralegals feel that medium-size law firms are the best of the lot. They offer the resources of large firms and the flexibility of small firms. A NALA survey released in 1995 showed that from 1993 to 1995, the greatest area of paralegal job growth was in firms with between two and thirty attorneys. Since paralegal turnover in these firms is lower than in the others, these jobs are generally harder to find.

Small Law Firms—Employer Summary

Characteristics: More likely to be a generalist when working in a variety of practice areas; less formal atmosphere.

Advantages: Greater job satisfaction reported by paralegals working in smaller firms; salaries often higher and more negotiable than in large firms; paralegals often involved in cases from beginning to end, unlike counterparts in larger firms.

Disadvantages: Fewer resources; no in-house training or paralegal manager; job descriptions might include administrative and/or clerical functions.

Whatever the size, there's a big difference between working in law firms and working in a corporation or government agency, and this difference is known as billable hours. The concept of billable hours exists only in law firms, which can make them more of a pressure cooker. However, the positive side to this is that, for the most part, a law firm's environment is more stimulating than a corporation's. In a law firm, you work on a variety of cases with a variety of clients. In a corporation, you work for only one client—the corporation.

CORPORATIONS

While corporations are the second-largest employer of paralegals, only 15 percent of paralegals find jobs in them. Examples of corporations that employ paralegals include technology companies, banks, insurance companies, brokerage firms, and manufacturing companies. In a corporation's organizational structure, the legal department usually reports directly to the chief executive officer.

An in-house legal department may have only a single attorney or over 100 of them, but the majority have one to twenty attorneys on their staff. The head of the legal department is the general counsel, who may also serve as the corporate secretary. (The title of corporate secretary may be misleading, since the corporate secretary is an officer of the company, right up there with the president and chief financial officer; it is not a clerical position. In some companies, the corporate secretary is a nonlawyer.) Under the general counsel, there are various levels of attorneys, including associate general counsel, assistant general counsel, senior counsel, and counsel. Depending on its size and needs, a legal department may or may not use paralegals.

Since most legal departments are too small to handle all the legal work of their corporations, they usually work closely with one or more outside firms. The amount of legal work given to outside counsel depends on the expertise of the corporation's in-house legal staff as well as its budgetary constraints. (Corporations are becoming more cost conscious when it comes to their legal bills. As you now know, outside counsel can get pretty expensive.)

A paralegal position in a corporation is significantly different from one in a law firm. One apparent difference—no billable hours—has already been mentioned. After working in a law firm, this can be quite a relief! The second major difference is that there's only one client to keep track of instead of many. As was previously mentioned, while a law firm environment may be stimulating, the pace in the corporation is slow and the pressure is less than in a law firm. This can be great for your mental health!

Another significant difference lies in the responsibilities of paralegals. In a corporation you might be responsible for more business and administrative tasks and less legal research. Even within the same specialty area, the tasks performed by a paralegal in a corporation can be quite different from those performed by a paralegal in a law firm.

For instance, one of my jobs as a paralegal in a corporation was to administer the company's stock option program, which falls under the legal specialty known as employee benefits. Stock options are a benefit given to key employees and involve the right to buy the company's stock at some time in the future, with luck at a price lower than the market value. Administering the program was very detailed and involved. Before working at the corporation, I had worked in the area of stock options at a law firm where the work involved drafting the agreements for the stock option plans. As you can see, the legal specialty area was the same— employee benefits—but the tasks were totally different.

Among the benefits of working at a corporation is the opportunity to learn about other areas of business, such as finance, accounting, and marketing. There are also more opportunities for advancement, since you can apply for positions in other departments. (This is one way to use your paralegal experience as a stepping-stone to other careers, as is discussed in more detail in Chapter 8.) Corporate salaries and benefits are usually better than those in law firms, although there are always exceptions. In addition, tuition reimbursement may be included in the benefits package and is a great way to help finance an advanced degree unrelated to law. (Law firms usually provide reimbursement only for seminars and continuing education courses that are directly related to your legal specialty.)

On the downside, positions in corporations are hard to come by. Most hire only paralegals with some law firm experience.

While corporations offer higher salaries, less stressful environments, and no billable hours, they may not offer the same kind of stimulation and on-the-job variety as law firms.

Corporations—Employer Summary

Characteristics: Employ 15 percent of all paralegals; includes for-profit corporations, banks, and insurance companies; no billable hours; work often includes more business-related than law-related tasks; work for one client as opposed to many.

Advantages: No billable hours; overtime not as likely; opportunity to move into other departments within company; better benefits.

Disadvantages: Generally need law firm experience to be hired; salary sometimes lower than in law firms; no opportunity to work for multiple clients.

GOVERNMENT

An alternative to working in a law firm or corporation is a position in a federal, state, or local government agency. Paralegals are employed in federal agencies such as the U.S. Department of Justice, Interstate Commerce Commission, Securities and Exchange Commission, and Federal Trade Commission; in state agencies and offices of state attorneys general; and in district attorney, public defender, and city attorney offices.

In 1975, the federal government developed two job classifications for paralegals: paralegal specialist and legal clerk/technician. Paralegal specialist is considered to be a professional-level job that guarantees career mobility and tenure. This job is analogous to the job of a paralegal in a private practice that specializes in a particular area. The legal clerk/technician position is similar to a case assistant and is more clerical by nature.

The tasks performed by government paralegals, particularly in the areas of civil and criminal litigation, are similar to those performed by their counterparts in the private sector, including legal and factual research, document analysis/organization, and trial preparation. Public sector paralegals also have tasks indigenous to government law practice involving regulatory and licensing procedures, administrative hearings, and legislative monitoring.

Before starting her own paralegal placement agency in Minneapolis, Denise Templeton worked in the office of Minnesota's attorney general. "I headed its new charitable trust division and was pleasantly surprised," she says. "I expected to find typical state government work attitudes in the employees, but instead they were some of the most motivated people I had ever worked with. The work was very interesting, and I was lucky to be able to work in that particular department. How interesting the government work is really depends on the particular agency you work for. I believe government is a growing sector for paralegal employment. City and county governments are starting to hire experienced paralegals instead of bringing employees up through the ranks and calling them something else."

There are other jobs in the federal government that involve paralegal-type work but are not classified that way. They include research analysts at the Federal Trade Commission, equal employment specialists at the Equal Employment Opportunity Commission, and procurement specialists at the Department of Defense. Positions such as these present excellent advancement opportunities.

In 1985, an enlightening study on the employment of paralegals in the offices of attorneys general around the nation was conducted by Nancy L. Helmich and Roger A. Larson with the cooperation of the National Association of Attorneys General (NAAG) and the University of Minnesota. Its purpose was to help publicize paralegal career opportunities in public service and to encourage paralegal educational programs to develop curricula in the area of public-sector employment. It showed that paralegals worked in such diverse areas as agriculture, civil rights, consumer affairs, criminal law, education, environmental affairs, health, labor, natural resources, public safety, taxation, transportation, and welfare, to name a few.

Perhaps the most interesting aspect of the study was its information on the reasons paralegals chose public-sector jobs. A common answer was interest in public affairs and issues related to government service.

Others included the challenge and variety offered by public service and the opportunity to help people and serve the public.

While a paralegal position in a government agency may be interesting, it should be noted that less than 5 percent of all paralegals work in this capacity. There are several reasons for this. The most obvious concerns the problem of bureaucratic red tape. Any government job involves extensive civil service procedures that have to be followed. Sometimes this results in long delays in hiring, which can be quite frustrating. Second, since the government doesn't bill clients for services, the argument for cost effectiveness that's used for paralegals in the private sector doesn't apply. And, because only a small number of paralegals are employed in the public sector, their talents and skills are likely to be underutilized by the attorneys who work with them.

Career Tip

Because of the cutbacks in federal funds to state and local governments, you're more likely to secure a job with a federal agency than with a state or local government agency. Overall, federal jobs are more stable than those on the state or local levels.

If the government is to continue providing low-cost legal services to the poor, the elderly, and others, it is apparent that both lawyers and paralegals need to focus greater attention on the role of paralegals in public service. In addition, more paralegal training programs should include courses on the public-sector paralegal. There is some irony in the fact that, while less than 5 percent of all paralegals are employed by the government, the government, as an industry, was the first to recognize the benefits of using them.

For anyone considering a paralegal position with the federal government, I recommend obtaining a copy of a pamphlet entitled *The Paralegal's Guide to U.S. Government Jobs: How to Land a Job in 140 Law-Related Careers,* available from Federal Reports, Inc., in Washington, D.C., at 202-393-3311. It provides detailed information on the pros and cons of federal employment and on the application and hiring process. It also contains a list of agencies, job titles, and salary ranges.

As more and more government agencies come to recognize the value of using paralegals, opportunities for paralegal employment in the public sector will increase. Nevertheless, due to the nature of our legal system, the greatest number of paralegal jobs will continue to be found in law firms.

Government—Employer Summary

Characteristics: Employs 5 percent of all paralegals; jobs available at the state, local, and federal levels.

Advantages: Greater paralegal job satisfaction reported; opportunity to work in areas not available in law firms, such as education and transportation; greater job stability.

Disadvantages: More bureaucracy in obtaining jobs; lower salaries tied to civil service.

OTHER ORGANIZATIONS

In recent years, paralegals have found jobs in nonprofit agencies, legal clinics, group legal services, consumer groups, and paralegal service companies—all thanks to the demand for affordable legal services and the increased recognition of paralegals by employers other than law firms and corporations.

Paralegal service companies are a recent phenomenon. They are usually owned and operated exclusively by paralegals or former paralegals. They provide legal support for law firms in such areas as civil litigation and family, probate, corporate, business, and bankruptcy law; employment opportunities for recent paralegal graduates; and internship possibilities for students currently enrolled in paralegal programs.

If such alternative employment opportunities appeal to you, before you pursue any of them keep in mind that the salary level for paralegal positions in these organizations is generally substantially lower than in law firms, corporations, and government agencies. Moreover, less than 5 percent of paralegals find positions in such organizations. Let's hope that this will change as the legal industry creates alternative methods for the delivery of cost-effective legal services.

Now that several kinds of paralegal employers have been discussed, the next two chapters will examine the job responsibilities and duties of paralegals in the major legal specialty areas.

Other Organizations—Employer Summary

Characteristics: Employs 5 percent of all paralegals; includes non-profit organizations, consumer groups, and paralegal companies.

Advantages: Greater job satisfaction because of the nature of the work.

Disadvantages: Salaries substantially lower than those at law firms and corporations.

CHAPTER 3

What Do Paralegals Do?
Four Traditional Practice Areas

The successful people are the ones who can think up stuff for the rest of the world to keep busy at.
Don Marquis

■

A paralegal sits cross-legged on the floor of a large room that's stacked to the ceiling with dozens of boxes. The boxes are filled with thousands of documents. Head bent, the paralegal is stamping the documents and preparing an index of each box.

This image of a paralegal poring over a roomful of endless documents is outdated and changing. It's been replaced by the vision of a new, more sophisticated paralegal performing tasks that were once the exclusive domain of attorneys.

The tasks paralegals perform depend in large part on the legal practice areas they work in, which, in turn, ultimately determine job satisfaction. The four areas of law that employ 90 percent of all paralegals are litigation, corporate, real estate, and probate.

Before looking at each specialty, some background on the law and the way our legal system is set up might be helpful in order to provide you with a framework for discussing the various specialty areas.

THE LAW IN BRIEF

Laws are the principles that govern conduct, protect rights, and define responsibilities. They serve three basic functions in our society by resolving disputes, maintaining order, and providing a basis for the transactions that occur in our daily lives.

Much of the law in the United States is based on the legal principles that were in effect under British rule—called common law—before the

American Revolution. The U.S. legal system is composed of four layers of law: constitutional law, statutory law, case law, and administrative law.

Laws are made through amendments to the U.S. Constitution and to the constitutions of each of the fifty states (constitutional law); through the passage of statutes by the U.S. Congress and by state and local legislatures (statutory law); through decisions made in federal, state, and local courts (case law); and through the passage of rules, regulations, orders, and decisions, such as Internal Revenue Service rulings, by federal, state, and local administrative agencies (administrative law).

Case law is a written opinion that explains a court decision and is based on precedent—the idea that what came before affects what comes after. A court uses precedent when, after applying specific legal principles to a case with a certain set of facts, it adheres to those principles by applying them in the future to cases with substantially the same facts.

Cases may be argued in three levels of court. The first level is trial court. In it, a case is heard, its facts are determined by the judge or jury, and law is applied to those facts by the judge. (In a jury trial, however, the judge would instruct the jury as to what legal principles it should apply.) Once the law is applied, a judgment is made.

If the judgment is appealed by either of the parties in the case (appeals can be made only on questions of law), the matter goes to the next level of court—an appellate court. The appellate court determines whether the ruling and judgment of the trial court were correct, and it issues an opinion.

If either of the parties wishes to appeal this opinion, the case is forwarded to a supreme, or high, court. The high court reviews the determination of the appellate court and issues an opinion that affirms or rejects the appellate decision.

Other special courts also exist at federal, state, and local levels. These include Tax Court, Court of Patent Appeals, Small Claims Court, Probate Court, Family Court, and Juvenile Court.

I hope that this information will make it easier for you to understand how different aspects of the law relate to the various practice areas and, ultimately, how they affect the duties and responsibilities of paralegals in those fields.

Before discussing each of the four traditional practice areas, you should be aware of the differences between two kinds of law that will make a tremendous amount of difference in your paralegal career.

Areas of Law in Which Most Paralegals Work

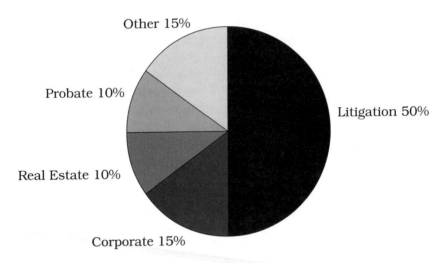

Other 15%

Probate 10%

Litigation 50%

Real Estate 10%

Corporate 15%

Court-Related v. Transactional Specialties

For most people, hearing the words law and lawyer conjures up strong images of lawsuits, trials, juries, and judges. Seldom do they think of the side of the law that doesn't revolve around the courtroom. As was mentioned earlier, the purpose of some laws is to provide a framework for regulating the transactions of daily life. Thus, transactional specialty areas such as corporate, real estate, intellectual property, and labor law are just as much a part of the legal profession as court-related specialties such as litigation. They cover matters such as incorporation, mergers and acquisitions, real estate purchases and sales, wills, estate management, workers' compensation, and trademark registration, to name a few. For the most part, they don't involve litigation, courtrooms, or lawsuits. One thing is for sure, though: they do provide many good employment opportunities for paralegals.

Career Tip

This distinction between court-related versus transactional areas is important for you to know when beginning your job search. Many paralegals become dissatisfied and leave the profession without ever realizing that they might have been happier working in a different specialty.

In 1981, after a year of working in civil litigation at a large San Francisco law firm, I knew litigation wasn't for me. It occurred to me that there was only so much I could do as a paralegal in that field. Furthermore, I wasn't too thrilled with the adversarial nature of it. After making my feelings known to the firm's paralegal manager, I switched into the securities and corporate group. The difference in jobs was like night and day. I no longer had to deal with courts, trials, or deposition summaries. For the next eight years, I worked exclusively in various nonlitigation areas. I've never regretted the move.

Before looking at the differences between each specialty area, you should know that no matter what area you work in, there are certain responsibilities common to all paralegals.

Common Paralegal Assignments

Whether you work in a court-related specialty such as litigation or a transactional area such as real estate, the majority of your time will be spent performing the responsibilities explained.

Career Tip

Your specific assignments will vary greatly depending on your experience, how much responsibility the attorney you work for is willing to delegate to you, the type of cases you work on, the specialty area you work in, and the type of employer that you work for.

Organizing documents. Make no mistake about it. Paralegal work is document intensive. You will spend approximately 50 percent of your time working with documents in some way. Entry-level paralegals usually spend more time summarizing, organizing, and managing documents than drafting or analyzing them, as does an experienced paralegal.

Drafting documents. The types of documents you prepare depend on your specialty area. For example, a corporate paralegal might draft a purchase and asset agreement, while a litigation paralegal might draft a set of questions (interrogatories) to the opposing counsel. A lot depends on how much the attorney trusts your writing abilities. Usually they're willing to let you take a crack at the first draft of a document, knowing that they'll have to prepare the final anyway.

Coordination. You'll spend a lot of time acting as a liaison between clients, attorneys, courts, and agencies, making sure things run smoothly. Approximately 20 percent of your time will be devoted to this. Remember that while the attorney is the strategist, it's up to the paralegal to know how to get the job done. One aspect of this that most paralegals find interesting and enjoyable is talking to clients. You'll be dealing with many clients at once, particularly if you're working in a law firm. I've found that, for the most part, clients would rather speak to a paralegal than to an attorney.

Factual research. Information gathering, fact-finding, and investigating is a large part of paralegal work and will account for about 20 percent of your time. Once again, your specialty area will dictate the type of factual research you'll be doing. For instance, as a corporate paralegal, I spent a lot of time searching computer databases for information on companies and their officers and directors.

Administrative tasks. Depending on the size of the law firm, you might have some nonbillable responsibilities related to office management, such as maintaining a calendar system or assisting in administering the law library. Most paralegals will also spend a few hours a week reviewing legal periodicals and other material relevant to their specialty area in order to keep up to date on the latest laws and regulations.

Legal research. The amount and type of legal research assignments given to paralegals depends in large part on the specialty area they work in and how much the attorney trusts their abilities. Legal research is quite different from factual research because there is a specific methodology to learn that takes some time.

Whenever I speak to someone considering a paralegal career, they assume that the majority of a paralegal's time is spent doing legal research. This is just not so. Due to the misconceptions surrounding legal research, this area of paralegal responsibility deserves special mention.

LEGAL RESEARCH EXPLAINED

Conducting legal research isn't difficult—it just takes some getting used to. Its foundation is the search for authorities in the law that are applicable to the facts of a particular legal problem or situation. The authorities are used to make an argument in court.

Authorities are found in either primary or secondary sources. Primary sources are actual laws: statutes passed by federal, state, and local legislatures (found in code books); court decisions (found in case books that are also known as reports or reporters); and administrative rules, regulations, and decisions. Secondary authorities aren't law. They're statements about the law and consist of two types: (1) books of search, such as encyclopedias, legal periodicals, and textbooks that explain or describe the law; and (2) books of index, such as digests, form books, tables, and dictionaries that are used to locate the law.

The search for authorities always begins with a search for mandatory primary sources, that is, constitutional, statutory, or case law of the same jurisdiction as your case. If these can't be found, then the search moves to persuasive primary sources—court decisions from other jurisdictions.

Legal research involves three steps: (1) determining the relevant facts in a case; (2) determining the legal issues involved; and (3) searching the law on the subject.

The TARP rule is used to determine which facts are relevant. This rule involves four factors: (1) **T**hing or subject matter; (2) cause of **A**ction or ground of defense; (3) **R**elief sought; and (4) **P**arties involved. After the facts are analyzed using this rule, the legal issues can be ascertained. Once this is done, the law can be searched for the authorities that are applicable to the facts in the case.

Finding the Law

Without going into a lot of detail, there are four methods for searching the law: (1) subject index approach; (2) topic or analytic method using issues and points of law in a problem; (3) case method used when the name of a case is known; and (4) word and phrase approach.

The third method of searching the law, the case method, is very common. A case is customarily referred to in terms of volume, source, and page number. The notation used to indicate these terms is called the cite (short for citation) and looks like this:

Ullman v. United States, 350 U.S. 422 (1956)

Deciphered, this cite means Ullman is the plaintiff; United States is the defendant; 350 is the volume number; U.S. is the abbreviation for the title of the publication, in this case, *United States Supreme Court Reports*;

422 is the page on which the case is found; and 1956 is the year it was decided. Once you become familiar with this reference system, locating cases is easy.

As stated earlier, case law is the written opinion that explains a decision made by a court. For research purposes, it can be found in either official reports published or authorized by the government or unofficial reports published by a private legal publishing company. The most popular unofficial publication of federal, regional, and state opinions is called *West's National Reporter System*. West has devised a unique key numbering system that it uses for all its publications. With it, legal principles are broken down into subject areas and subcategories and assigned key numbers. Related cases are correspondingly referenced under the same numbers. Because key number assignments are used in all of West's publications, they can help to locate cases that pertain to a particular subject or legal principle easily throughout the *West's National Reporter System*.

Administrative agency decisions, opinions, rules, and regulations are published by private legal publishers in what are known as loose-leaf reports. (They are so named because they consist of separate, individual pages that can be inserted and removed from loose-leaf binders.) Commerce Clearing House (CCH) publishes various loose-leaf reports on tax law. Matthew Bender is another well-known legal publisher of loose-leaf reports. These reports also cite statutes and case law.

Shepardizing—Is the Law Valid?

Suppose you have found five cases that support a client's argument. Or do they? How do you know if these cases are still law or whether they were reversed or overruled last month by an appellate or high court? Have the courts followed the principles of law established in the case? Before you can use a case as authority for the client's argument, you need to know how it was treated by the courts. The method for doing that is called *Shepardizing*, named after Frank Shepard, who invented the system in 1873.

Shepard's Citations, published by Shepard's/McGraw-Hill, is a set of books that includes cases, federal and state statutes, administrative agency rulings, and material from legal periodicals. Through a notation system that takes some getting used to, *Shepard's Citations* provides the history of a case (whether it was affirmed, dismissed, modified, reversed, or vacated) and its treatment (whether it was explained, followed, overruled, or questioned). *Shepardizing* is usually done by paralegals, although some attorneys prefer to do it themselves.

While a detailed discussion of how to *Shepardize* is beyond the scope of this book, suffice it to say that *Shepardizing* is one of the most essential tools of legal research. The consequences of improper *Shepardizing* can be devastating. Imagine an attorney walking into a courtroom only to find out that the cases he or she used in order to prepare—the cases you *Shepardized*—have been reversed. I've seen it happen.

Legal Research Assignments

The kinds of legal research done by paralegals vary widely, depending on the practice area they are in. Assignments for entry-level paralegals working in litigation are often limited to locating, copying, cite checking, and *Shepardizing* cases. With more experience, a paralegal is often asked to research a problem to find cases "on point" that either help or hinder a client's arguments. But since this type of substantive research can either make or break a case, some attorneys prefer to do it themselves. Experienced paralegals are sometimes asked to prepare a memorandum of law, which is a detailed analysis of the facts and legal issues in a case.

Litigation paralegals are not the only ones who perform legal research. Paralegals working in transactional areas such as real estate, securities, tax, and patent law often refer to administrative agency decisions, opinions, rules, and regulations that are published in loose-leaf reports.

Most paralegals are expected to know both the traditional methods of legal research discussed so far, as well as computer-assisted legal research methods using LEXIS and WESTLAW legal databases and CD-ROMs as well as legal research sites on the Internet. These methods will be discussed at length in Chapter 6. Much of the work that was done manually such as cite checking and *Shepardizing* are now done using computer databases, CD-ROMs, and the Internet.

FOUR TRADITIONAL PRACTICE AREAS

Since the majority of paralegals work in one or more of the four primary specialties—litigation, corporate, real estate, or probate—our answer to the question What do paralegals do? will begin here. Keep in mind that oftentimes paralegals will work in more than one area simultaneously, particularly if they work for a small law firm.

Top 10 Substantive Tasks Performed by Paralegals
Assist with labor negotiations
Assist at trial; trial preparation
Complete audit letters
Computerized litigation support
Corporate organization
Estate administration
Legal research
Prepare motions; briefs; memorandums of law
Prepare settlement packages; petitions
Prepare real estate closings
Source: Copyright © 1997 James Publishing, Inc. Reprinted courtesy of *Legal Assistant Today* magazine. For subscription information, call (800) 394-2626.

In order to discuss the responsibilities of each practice area, it's necessary for me to use legal terms and concepts that may be unfamiliar to you. It isn't my intention to bog you down with terminology but rather to introduce the terms to you as some of the things paralegals should know. However, if you have difficulty with any terms, there are several good legal dictionaries and paralegal handbooks available that will define them.

LITIGATION

Since dispute resolution is the most common function of law in our legal system, it should come as no surprise that more than half of all paralegals work in litigation. Litigation associated with the year 2000 "bug" alone is expected to range anywhere from several hundred million dollars to $1 trillion. (This bug is predicted to cause computers to malfunction due to outdated software code written in the 1960s that only allows the computer to read the year 2000 as a double digit "00."

Litigation refers to a controversy in which all parties agree to have their legal rights determined and enforced in court. In a strict technical sense, the term refers to civil actions and not to criminal actions. Two kinds of cases often brought to court are criminal and civil. They represent two major kinds of law. The responsibilities discussed in this section relate to civil cases.

Civil law is designed to protect citizens as private individuals in their relationships with one another. The majority of civil lawsuits revolve around contracts or torts. A contract is a written or unwritten agreement (a promise or set of promises) between two or more parties. A tort—a wrong or injury to a person or damage to property—is the principle through which the injured party can collect monetary compensation from the person who caused the harm. Most torts involve wrongdoing to individuals under civil law, although torts do arise from criminal actions, such as assault and battery.

What Is a Lawsuit?

Since nearly all of the duties performed by litigation paralegals revolve around lawsuits, a little background on the processes and procedures is necessary. There are four stages to a lawsuit: commencement of an action (complaint and answer), discovery, trial, and appeal.

The first phase begins when one party files a complaint against another. The complaint is the first statement (or pleading) prepared by whoever is initiating the lawsuit (the plaintiff), and it deals with the nature and basis of the lawsuit (the grounds). Its purpose is to notify the adversary, or defendant, of the grounds for the suit. The defendant then prepares an answer in response, which contains denials of the allegations made by the plaintiff. A law firm would represent either the plaintiff or the defendant.

The second phase is called discovery. This is where both parties literally discover facts and information about the other in order to prepare for trial. There are various tools used for discovery, but the four most common are:

- *Interrogatories*—A fancy term for written questions

- *Depositions*—Statements made under oath in a question-and-answer format

- *Requests for production of documents*—A request by one party that the other party produce documents for it and make them available for inspection and photocopying

- *Requests for admissions*—Written statements that positively affirm or deny facts or allegations at issue in the case. (These serve two purposes: to uncover facts and to resolve some issues before going to trial.)

The third phase, the trial, is an examination of the issues and facts of a case in a court that has jurisdiction over it. Trial procedures include jury selection (if it's a trial by jury), the attorneys' opening statements, the plaintiff's presentation of evidence, the defendant's objections, the defendant's presentation of evidence, the plaintiff's objections, submission of the case to a jury, instructions to the jury, the verdict, and order of the court.

The fourth stage of a lawsuit is the appeal to a higher court. Both the plaintiff and the defendant have the right to file an appeal—within a specified time period—if not satisfied with the verdict. The purpose of the appeal is to obtain a review of a lower court's decision and a reversal of the judgment or a new trial. The appellate court bases its decision primarily on the attorneys' written pleadings and not on their oral arguments.

The Litigation Paralegal's Job

To reiterate, the tasks performed by any paralegal vary greatly, depending on the type of organization, the size of the case, the complexity of the legal issues, the level of the paralegal's experience, and the attitude of the attorney supervising the paralegal. The tasks discussed here are typical for paralegals working on small- to medium-size civil litigation cases at law firms that involve paralegals in cases from beginning to end. (It's worth noting that paralegals hired to work on large, complex cases often work only on discovery. Since discovery on these kinds of cases can take years, it's common for a paralegal to change jobs or leave the firm before the case ever goes to trial.)

Commencement of an action. In the first phase of a lawsuit—the commencement of an action—a paralegal would be responsible for:

- Performing investigation and analysis of the facts of the case;
- Organizing and analyzing client documents;
- Preparing chronologies of facts in the case;
- Drafting or assisting in drafting the complaint or answer (if representing the plaintiff or defendant, respectively);
- Setting up and maintaining a calendar system; and
- Performing legal or factual research.

Discovery. Because the discovery phase of a lawsuit produces so many documents, paralegals spend most of their time organizing, analyzing, indexing, and filing. Depending on the size of the case and the resources of the law firm, this is either done manually or with the assistance of litigation support software and computers. However, more often than not you will be required to learn and use litigation support software. It is the rare firm these days that does not rely to some extent on computer technology to assist in the discovery process. Some of a paralegal's responsibilities during the discovery phase include:

- Preparing interrogatories, requests for production of documents, and requests for admissions and/or responses to these documents;

- Drafting motions (formal requests to the judge relating to issues that arise during the lawsuit);

- Locating, interviewing, and obtaining witness statements;

- Drafting deposition questions;

- Supervising a computerized litigation support system (if applicable);

- Summarizing depositions;

- Managing document productions; and

- Organizing files and analyzing documents.

Of all these tasks, summarizing depositions and managing document productions are the most time-consuming. A deposition summary is a summary, in the summarizer's own words, of testimony taken in a deposition. For instance, the attorney you've been assigned to has spent the last three days taking Mr. Doe's deposition. A transcript of it has been typed up by a court reporter and is 500 pages long. It would be too time-consuming for the attorney to read through all 500 pages to prepare for trial, so you're responsible for condensing it into a 40-page summary. (On average, it takes an hour to summarize 15 pages of transcript.)

Deposition summaries can be nearly unmanageable when hundreds of volumes of transcripts need to be summarized. In these cases, depositions are sometimes sent out to a deposition summary service. I've found that due to the confidential nature of the testimony, some firms prefer to have their own paralegals do the summaries. Summarizing hundreds of volumes is an enormous task and often leads to very frustrated paralegals. In the past few years, the availability of new litigation support software products has greatly minimized the tedium of these tasks.

The other task that takes up a lot of time is preparing for document productions. A document production is a legal device used by both sides of a suit to discover the facts in a case.

For example, let's say that the firm you work for is representing the IBM Corporation, the plaintiff in a case. Your attorney has just received a request from the defendant for all of IBM's documents that refer in any way to the Xerox Corporation from 1970 to 1984. It's your job as a paralegal to go through all of the documents that have been received from the client, locate the ones that refer to Xerox in that time period, and make them available to the defendant for inspection. It's likely that you'd have to examine thousands of documents to complete a task like this, and it's possible that it would take hundreds of hours.

A time will be set for the defendant's attorney to inspect the documents (usually at your firm). After the attorney has decided which document he or she wants, you would arrange for copies of those documents to be made and sent to that attorney's office. (If you were a paralegal working for the defendant, once your attorney received those documents, you would be responsible for stamping them with a Bates number, putting them in chronological order, and preparing an index of all the documents.) No matter what side of the case you're working for, managing documents is time consuming.

Nowadays discovery requests might include something called "electronic discovery." This means that the attorney is asked for computer-generated evidence in the form of floppy disks, hard drives, CD-ROMs and other electronic media. In such situations a computer-savvy paralegal can be invaluable.

Career Tip

Document requests continue throughout the discovery phase of the lawsuit. As a result, some of the larger cases have dozens of document productions. Once again, this is a frustrating job for some paralegals. And yet, discovery can be quite interesting, particularly in small cases where there are fewer depositions and documents to manage. Therefore, the size of the case is an important consideration when looking for your first paralegal job.

Trial. A paralegal's responsibilities during the trial phase of a lawsuit fall into three categories: pretrial, trial, and posttrial. Some of the assignments might include:

- *Pretrial*—Drafting legal documents such as briefs, pretrial statements, settlement conference memoranda, and jury instructions
—Reviewing briefs for accuracy of factual information
—shepardizing and cite checking
—Preparing trial exhibits and trial notebook
—Obtaining a list of jury members

- *Trial*—Coordinating the scheduling of witnesses
—Assisting in the preparation of witnesses
—Attending the trial and taking notes
—Maintaining a list of exhibits

- *Posttrial*—Summarizing trial testimony
—Preparing a bill of costs
—Drafting a motion for a new trial (if applicable)
—Managing posttrial collections work

Trials represent the culmination of months, sometimes years, of hard work and can be quite rewarding (if your side wins, of course). But they are also a time of tremendous stress; everyone puts in overtime.

Appeal. The final phase of the lawsuit, the appeal, is based primarily on the pleadings submitted by the attorneys and not on oral arguments. Since the majority of time required by a lawsuit is spent on discovery, very few paralegals ever perform appellate work.

"My job consisted of a great deal of trial work, document organization and control, and talking with codefendants and the plaintiff's counsel," says Engrid Tronsrue about her past experiences as a litigation paralegal in a large Denver, Colorado, law firm. "I loved going to trial. I worked with twenty-one plaintiffs and five codefendants on a products liability case that involved very complex medical issues. (Products liability cases typically involve claims that a product was defective—in some way due to negligent manufacture—and resulted in an injury.)

"I spent a lot of time working with expert witnesses, coordinating the scheduling of medical exams for the plaintiffs, as well as scheduling the depositions. Essentially, I made sure everything flowed smoothly and that the attorneys had what they needed. At that firm, most of the legal research was done by law clerks, but, with all the other responsibilities I had, I didn't miss it. What I enjoyed most was dealing with people, working with our investigator, and calling the expert witnesses myself and interviewing them."

This kind of involvement is considered by many paralegals to be one of the main advantages of working in litigation.

Litigation—Career Summary

Characteristics: Adversarial, court-related tasks; varied cases and clients, including civil, antitrust, and tort litigation (i.e., personal injury, product liability, and medical malpractice); document-intensive work; opportunity for sophisticated assignments and job satisfaction, depending on size of case.

Advantages: Employs 40 to 50 percent of all paralegals; good foundation for understanding law; excellent freelance potential; job satisfaction more likely working in smaller law firms on small cases from start to finish; large job market.

Disadvantages: Overtime most likely; high burnout rate, particularly when working on large cases in repetitive, document-intensive activities.

CORPORATE LAW

Approximately 15 percent of all paralegals work in corporate law. Since corporate law revolves around business-related transactions, paralegals in this specialty area rarely perform court-related tasks. (Depending on your personal preferences, this is either an advantage or a disadvantage.) Their work most often relates to general corporate work such as incorporations, ongoing corporate work, dissolutions and partnership matters, mergers and acquisitions, and securities law.

Incorporations

Incorporation is the legal process through which an association of owners creates a corporation; that is, it's a way of structuring a company. The process is governed by state statutes. The legal document that establishes a corporation is called the articles of incorporation. A corporation is considered an artificial person under the law and exists as a legal entity separate from the people who own it. Those people, the shareholders, elect directors to manage the affairs of the organization. The directors, in turn, appoint officers to run the day-to-day operations.

Corporate paralegals who work on an incorporation are responsible for:

- Determining the availability of the corporate name and reserving it with the secretary of state;
- Drafting and filing articles of incorporation;
- Drafting the bylaws, minutes of first meeting of the board of directors and shareholders, and answers for various federal and state forms;
- Preparing the minutes book, share certificates, stock transfer records, and qualifications for issuance of stock; and
- Obtaining appropriate licenses to operate specific businesses, such as a liquor store, a hotel, or a pharmacy, when necessary.

Ongoing Corporate Matters

The duties that are performed by paralegals and related to the ongoing maintenance of a corporation vary considerably, depending in large part on whether the paralegal works in a law firm or a corporation. For a paralegal working in a law firm, the tasks generally include:

- Drafting legal documents, such as employment agreements, shareholders' agreements, and stock option plans;
- Amending articles of incorporation and/or bylaws;
- Preparing notices, agendas, resolutions, and minutes for corporate activities that require the approval of directors and/or shareholders;
- Filing the qualifications for corporations to do business in other states;
- Maintaining corporate records of subsidiaries; and
- Preparing Uniform Commercial Code (UCC) filings. (The UCC is a set of laws that govern commercial transactions between states.)

In addition to these duties, paralegals who work for corporations may have responsibilities that revolve around the activities of the corporate secretary and board of directors. These include:

- Reporting the purchase and sale of stock by officers and directors;
- Preparing for board of directors meetings;
- Calculating dividend record and payable dates;
- Administering executive stock option programs and dividend reinvestment plans;
- Drafting proxy statements and 10-K forms;
- Managing shareholder relations programs and proxy solicitations;

- Supervising the stock transfer agent; and
- Coordinating the annual meeting of shareholders.

Corporate Dissolutions

There are several reasons for dissolving corporations. One is when the tax laws change to favor other forms of ownership such as partnerships. A more obvious reason is when a corporation becomes insolvent and can no longer carry on its business profitability. Corporate paralegals who work on dissolving corporations are assigned to draft, file, and obtain documents in connection with:

- Certificates of election to wind up and dissolve;
- Statements of intent to dissolve, articles of dissolution, and other required state forms to effect dissolution;
- Notices to creditors;
- Tax clearances;
- Withdrawals of qualifications to do business in other states;
- State and federal tax dissolution forms;
- Distribution of corporate assets; and
- Cancellation of share certificates.

Partnerships and Limited Liability Companies

As mentioned earlier, a partnership is another way to structure a company. It is a mutual agreement, either written or verbal, between two or more persons to carry on a business for profit. The most common type of partnership is a limited partnership. It consists of one or more general partners who manage the partnership and limited partners who only contribute capital. Limited partners don't participate in the operation or management of the partnership and are liable only for the amount of their investment.

In recent years two new types of organizational structures have gained in popularity: limited liability companies (LLCs) and limited liability partnerships (LLPs). An LLC is a hybrid—something between a partnership and a corporation. It combines the "pass through" tax treatment of a partnership with the limited liability afforded corporate shareholders. An LLP is a general partnership, primarily formed by professionals like doctors, lawyers, and accountants, that shields the partners from liability, affords them full partnership tax treatment, and allows them to operate with less formality and more flexibility than a corporation.

The duties of paralegals within the area of partnerships and LLCs vary depending on the law at any given time. For instance, in the early 1980s, when tax laws favored partnerships, I found myself spending 80 percent of my time working on partnership transactions. When the tax laws changed, I spent most of my time preparing incorporations.

In partnership and LLC transactions, a paralegal's responsibilities might include:

- Checking name availability and reserving or registering partnership or LLC name;
- Drafting certificates of limited partnership;
- Drafting limited partnership agreements and amendments;
- Drafting certificates of formation and management agreements for LLCs;
- Preparing, filing, and recording statements of partnership and certificates of limited partnership;
- Preparing, filing, and publishing fictitious business name statements (if the partnership is to operate under an assumed name and not under the partners' actual names) and notices of termination of partnership;
- Drafting partnership and LLC annual reports and state filings;
- Maintaining partnership and LLC records; and
- Drafting minutes of partnership meetings and agreements for dissolution of partnership.

Mergers and Acquisitions

Due to the wave of corporate takeovers that occurred in the mid-1980s and their resurgence in the mid-1990s, the attorneys and paralegals who work on these transactions develop specialized knowledge in the area of mergers and acquisitions (also known as M&A). The responsibilities of a paralegal who works in mergers and acquisitions might include:

- Assisting in drafting letters of intent;
- Preparing drafts of merger, purchase, and sale agreements;
- Participating in due diligence investigations;
- Drafting employment contracts and closing documents; and

- Obtaining UCC filing clearances and good standing certificates.

Kathy Allen, a former paralegal at a large law firm in Atlanta, Georgia, worked in M&A. Note her career path and educational background; it's typical of those who work in this area of corporate law:

"I started in general corporate and gradually moved into securities work, particularly in the area of mergers and acquisitions. I did a great deal of research to make sure the company was qualified to do business in all the states. I also performed due diligence, which is done when a company becomes public or is involved in an acquisition. It consisted of reviewing company records to make sure they are in proper order and that the company is in good standing. I found my bachelor's degree in finance to be useful, particularly when doing due diligence, reading annual reports, and helping attorneys interpret the financial status of a particular company."

One final note about M&A work: it's a subspecialty of corporate and securities law, and paralegal jobs in it are few and far between.

Securities Law

Securities law involves the sale and purchase of securities—stocks, bonds, preferred stocks, debentures, and options—for the purpose of raising capital.

Most of the assignments for paralegals in this area relate to initial stock offerings; secondary stock, bond, or limited partnership offerings; private placement offerings; reporting requirements of securities trading; and the registration of securities with the state, called "blue-sky" law. What a securities law paralegal does on a day-to-day basis depends on where he or she works. A paralegal in a law firm could work exclusively on initial stock offerings, while a paralegal in a corporation could spend the majority of the time preparing Securities and Exchange Commission (SEC) compliance filings. The responsibilities of a securities law paralegal might include some or all of the following:

- Drafting portions of the registration statement (a document that discloses the plans, objectives, and financial information of a company to potential purchasers of the company's securities);

- Preparing documents, such as questionnaires, for officers and directors, underwriting agreements, and preliminary blue-sky memoranda;

- Filing the registration statement and working with the financial printer;
- Preparing applications to register securities in various states and other blue-sky tasks;
- Preparing reports under the Securities Exchange Act of 1934, including proxy statements, 10-K and 10-Q forms, annual reports to shareholders, stock exchange listing applications, and insider trading reports;
- Assisting in preparation of private offering circulars; and
- Preparing for and attending private placement closings.

Career Tip

As I stated at the beginning of this chapter, after a year of litigation work, I switched over to securities law. I found it extremely interesting and challenging and recommend it to anyone who's interested in a long-term paralegal career.

Corporate Law—Career Summary

Characteristics: Transactional specialty involving business-related tasks; employs 15 percent of all paralegals; subspecialties include mergers and acquisitions and securities law involving financial and investment matters; tasks vary greatly depending on whether working in law firm or corporation.

Advantages: Not adversarial; high salary potential; less frenetic and stressful; sophisticated assignments; greater autonomy; subspecialties have higher salary potential than general corporate work; good foundation for other business-related careers; securities law and mergers and acquisitions subspecialties excellent for long-term paralegal career.

Disadvantages: Smaller job market than litigation; difficult to find jobs in corporations without law firm experience; some paralegals find general corporate work boring.

REAL ESTATE

Less than 10 percent of all paralegals work in real estate law. Real estate laws govern the ownership and transferability of real property. Real property refers to an interest in land or buildings, as distinguished from personal property, which refers to any transportable goods.

As a law practice area, real estate law involves one or more of the following activities: representation of the buyer or seller in commercial, residential, or industrial real estate purchases or sales; representation of the lender or borrower in real estate financings; representation of the landlord or tenant in leasehold matters; real estate litigation, if any; and the real estate aspects of corporate transactions.

Phases of a Real Estate Transaction

In a real estate transaction that involves the purchase, sale, or financing of property, there are four phases in which paralegals play an integral role. These are determining title, preparing for the closing, attending the closing, and the postclosing follow-up.

In the first phase, the primary concern is to determine the status of title to the property. Having title to something means having the right to possess it. Title to a property may be affected by certain rights, or encumbrances, upon the property by other individuals. One such right is called a lien, which is a claim upon the property as security for debt owed. A common type of lien is a mechanic's lien for the payment of money owed for labor, services, or material furnished in erecting or repairing a building on the property. (Many of the tasks performed by real estate paralegals center on the concept of title.)

In the second phase of a transaction, the paralegal's role is to coordinate all details to ensure a smooth closing. The tasks performed in this phase include drafting various closing documents such as deeds, mortgages, bills of sale, promissory notes, and assignments of lease; estimating closing costs; and working with the title company in clearing any objections to the title report. The closing, the third phase, is an interesting and rewarding time for paralegals, since it represents the culmination of hours of hard work. During the closing, the paralegal may manage all documents, obtain signatures, and work with the title company.

The final phase involves postclosing duties, which include preparation of a binder containing all closing documents and follow-up work with the title company.

Career Tip

Many of the tasks performed by paralegals in a real estate practice depend on whether the law firm represents the purchaser, seller, lender, or borrower. Other considerations are the type of property and the kind of transaction involved; these include single-family dwellings, condominiums, and industrial sites; commercial leases, partnerships, foreclosures, and financings; and landlord/tenant matters.

Real estate paralegals who work on a purchase, sale, or financing might be responsible for:

- Conducting title searches and updates;
- Preparing a preliminary abstract of title and an opinion on the title;
- Assisting clients to obtain mortgage financing and to record mortgages;
- Drafting, reviewing, and analyzing documents, such as truth-in-lending disclosure statements, easements, legal descriptions of property, deeds, leases, assignments, escrow instructions, and closing statements;
- Preparing formal lien clearances;
- Obtaining documents that relate to a borrower's financial condition;
- Conducting UCC searches;
- Preparing for and attending closings; and
- Performing postclosing work, such as obtaining canceled notes, deeds of trust, or title policies, and assisting clients in obtaining liability insurance.

In a corporate legal department, real estate paralegals may assist in employee relocation. The paralegal can aid in the sale and/or purchase of a home by coordinating the activities of real estate brokers, title companies, and real estate lawyers. In addition, since a corporation must file property tax returns for each state in which it has property, paralegals may maintain property ownership records, analyze tax assessments, assist in drafting the company's response to tax adjustments, and monitor tax legislation that affects the property.

In a corporation or a firm, the paralegals who specialize in real estate law often perform tasks similar to those who work in corporate law or litigation. For instance, when preparing a closing for a corporate client, a real estate paralegal might draft shareholder or director resolutions, tasks that are also done by corporate paralegals. The litigation-type duties in real estate law involve mortgage foreclosures, unlawful detainer actions (landlord/tenant disputes), and actions that determine who owns title to property.

"I really enjoyed working in real estate and believe it's an important area for paralegals to specialize in," says Peggy Ruse about her experiences as a real estate paralegal in a large San Francisco law firm. "I worked very independently and was given a lot of responsibility. Some of my duties were drafting documents, negotiating title insurance with title companies, and preparing for real estate closings. I became an expert in title insurance and found that attorneys rely very heavily on paralegals in this area. I might caution paralegals interested in this area that real estate paralegals often work long hours—particularly when preparing for and attending closings. Basically, you don't go home until the deal is done."

Peggy believes that real estate paralegals can advance into real estate development by working in commercial property sales and development.

Real Estate Law—Career Summary

Characteristics: Transactional specialty employing 10 percent of paralegals; few court-related tasks, except when case involves real estate litigation; requires a high level of responsibility; cases involve representation of buyer, seller, or lender in purchases, sales, or financings of residential, commercial, or industrial properties; opportunities in both law firms and corporations.

Advantages: Good area for long-term paralegal career, particularly when economy improves; high salary potential; good foundation for other real estate careers.

Disadvantages: Small job market; opportunities dependent on economy and real estate industry; currently, employment opportunities are increasing due to a resurgence in commercial and residential development and property values.

PROBATE

Less than 10 percent of all paralegals work in the specialty field of probate, which also includes the subspecialty of estate planning. Estate planning refers to the management and distribution of property, including wills, trusts, gifts, taxes, and investments. Probate is the legal process through which a court decides on the validity of a will, reviews its provisions, and orders the final disposition of the assets of the estate.

Estate Planning

The laws that govern the estate planning field deal with the disposition of real and personal property. Most people are familiar with the concept of a will—the traditional way of transferring property to heirs. A will is merely the declaration of a person's desires about how his or her property should be disposed of after death. Its purpose is to prevent the state from distributing the estate according to state laws. But there's more to estate planning than the preparation of a will. Other legal devices can be used to dispose of property or assets—among them trusts (property held by one person for the benefit of another) and outright gifts. These devices are not subject to probate procedures, which are often costly and time consuming.

The responsibilities of a paralegal employed in an estate planning practice might include:

- Analyzing client assets and financial information;
- Preparing tax calculations;
- Monitoring state statutes to ensure that estate plans conform to state law;
- Drafting legal documents such as wills, trust agreements, and documents that relate to trust funds;
- Preparing summaries of provisions of wills and trust agreements;
- Recording asset transfer documents;
- Completing trust registration and advising clients of notice requirements;
- Obtaining, reviewing, and analyzing insurance policies;
- Preparing change of beneficiary forms; and
- Updating wills to comply with changes in the laws.

Probate

Several types of matters are filed in probate court, including estate proceedings (of which there are two types: testate proceedings, in which a person dies and leaves a will, and intestate proceedings, in which no will is left). There are also conservatorships (in which a court appoints an individual to care for the property and/or person of someone determined to be unable to manage his or her own property) and guardianships (in which the court appoints an individual to care for the person and/or property of a minor).

The steps involved in a typical probate matter consist of holding the initial conference with the client or closest family member (if the client is deceased), commencing probate proceedings, taking inventory of the assets of the decedent's estate, valuating those assets, paying the decedent's debts and expenses, making an accounting to the court, filing tax returns (estate tax, inheritance tax, etc.), and, ultimately, distributing assets and closing the estate. In a probate proceeding, a paralegal's assignments might involve:

- Taking an inventory of the decedent's home;
- Opening the safe deposit box for burial instructions and/or the will;
- Locating witnesses to prove the authenticity of the will;
- Corresponding with institutions to obtain asset information;
- Obtaining copies of the death certificate;
- Publishing the death notice in newspapers;
- Preparing a petition for probate of the will;
- Filing claims for insurance proceeds and death benefits;
- Preparing disallowance of claims against the estate;
- Itemizing and appraising the value of estate assets;
- Preparing documents for the sale of assets;
- Paying debts, liens, and expenses;
- Preparing gift, estate, inheritance, and other tax returns;
- Requesting a final audit;
- Applying for release of estate assets;
- Preparing final and supplemental accountings; and
- Transferring assets to heirs.

Because the majority of tasks involve the preparation of tax returns, accountings, and asset valuations, probate paralegals must be fairly good with numbers. "For people who want to get into the probate area, I recommend an accounting class, as well as a class in investments," suggests Mary Beth Schultz, a probate, tax, and estates paralegal at a law firm in Minneapolis, Minnesota. "Also, a person should be detail oriented and enjoy working with numbers, since a lot of the work involves taxes and preparing final accountings for estates."

In terms of the practice, Mary Beth has noticed an increase in requests for estate planning, with a decrease in probate work, due to a trend by the general public to place more assets in trusts and joint tenancy.

Estate Planning/Probate—Career Summary

Characteristics: Transactional area, with some court-related duties; knowledge of accounting and investments helpful; employs less than 10 percent of paralegals; opportunities exist primarily in law firms; requires a high level of responsibility.

Advantages: Specialization area; good freelance opportunities; excellent salary potential.

Disadvantages: Small job market; difficult to break into.

This chapter has presented the four traditional areas of paralegal employment. Opportunities for paralegals in transactional specialties such as corporate and real estate law fluctuate with the health of the economy. But thanks to the litigious nature of our society, litigation is a cash cow for lawyers. As a result, chances are good that your first position will be in litigation.

For more detail on what paralegals do, I highly recommend obtaining a copy of *Paralegal Responsibilities* published by the National Federation of Paralegal Associations, Inc. at a nonmember cost of $15. The booklet lists responsibilities in the following areas: Appellate, Asbestos Litigation, Bankruptcy, Business/Corporate, Collections, Computer Litigation Support, Construction, Contract Administration, Criminal, Domestic Relations/Family Law, Employee Benefits, Environmental Law, Foreclose, Immigration, Intellectual Property, Labor/Employment, Landlord/Tenant, Litigation, Personal Injury/Medical Malpractice/Product Liability, Probate and Estate Administration, Public Benefits, Real Property, Securities/Municipal Bonds, Tax, and Workers' Compensation.

The whole point of this chapter as well as the next one is to make you aware of the fact that just because you start out in litigation does not mean that you have to stay in it. The specialty areas you'll read about in the next chapter are some of the fastest-growing fields and are the best prospects for paralegal employment in the next few years.

CHAPTER 4

"Hot" Paralegal Specialties

*Learn from the mistakes of others—you can't live long enough
to make them all yourself.*
Martin Vanbee

■

"Computer Experts Divided on Cost of Year-2000 Fix," "Sex Bias on Pay Alleged," "Unhealthy Pension Plans Pose Gamble for Workers," "Residents Feeling Effects of Toxic Spill," "Losses from Bankruptcies Take an Unexpected Jump."

The newspapers are filled with headlines such as these. Issues concerning technology, job discrimination, pension fraud, the environment, and business failures have increased the need for legal advice in the areas of intellectual property, labor and employment, employee benefits, environmental law, and bankruptcy. Growth in these areas is providing greater job opportunities for paralegals. If I were beginning a paralegal career today, I'd strongly consider working in one of these specialties, as well as the areas of immigration law and computerized litigation support.

"Hot" Specialties At A Glance

- ✔ Intellectual Property
- ✔ Computerized Litigation Support
- ✔ Employment and Labor Law
- ✔ Employee Benefits
- ✔ Environmental Law
- ✔ Bankruptcy
- ✔ Immigration

INTELLECTUAL PROPERTY

The field of intellectual property law has exploded in the past few years, presenting abundant opportunities for attorneys and paralegals alike.

The globalization of our economy and with it, the increase in multinational companies, has made intellectual property law, and, in particular, trademark and patent work, a fast-growing specialty. And, as a cost-containment measure, large corporations are more likely to keep trademark work in their in-house law departments, rather than hire outside counsel to do such work for them. This in turn means a growing need for paralegal support within corporations to handle the registration and management of trademarks. Trademark paralegals have substantial autonomy and client contact, handle international projects, and work with cutting-edge product and service technologies.

Thanks to the proliferation of multimedia and Internet companies, complicated issues arising from doing business on the Internet as well as the use of copyrighted material in multimedia CD-ROMs have increased the demand for legal services in this area.

And then there is the ill-fated year 2000 "bug," which, as you will recall from Chapter 3, will cause computers to malfunction due to outdated software code relating to dates written in the 1960s that only allows the computer to read the year 2000 as a double digit 00. Intellectual property attorneys everywhere are expected to keep busy with this problem as they review and revise clients' software license agreements.

As a practice area, intellectual property includes four broad categories: trademarks, patents, copyrights, and trade secrets. To understand the differences between the categories, you need only to refer to their respective bodies of law.

Trademark law is concerned with protecting the exclusive right of merchants and manufacturers to use any name, word, symbol, or device to identify their goods and/or services.

Patent law involves protecting an inventor's exclusive right to make, use, or sell his or her invention over a specified period of time.

Copyright law has to do with protecting the exclusive right of writers and artists to publish their creative works and with determining who may publish such works. Some examples of works protected by copyright law are music, art, literature, motion pictures, audiovisual works, sound recordings, and computer software.

Trade secrets law involves protecting a business's exclusive right to use and keep secret from competitors any formula, pattern, machine, or manufacturing process that gives the business a competitive advantage.

Intellectual property is a highly specialized field. The area of patents, for instance, requires knowledge of technical and scientific terms. Very few paralegals work exclusively in the area of intellectual property. Unless you're hired by a very large corporation or a law firm that specializes in intellectual property, you're likely to work in other practice areas of law as well. During my year as a litigation paralegal, for instance, I also worked on assignments that dealt with the trademark registration of a ski resort in Lake Tahoe, Nevada.

Given the nature of the intellectual property practice, most paralegal tasks center on three types of activities: the search to ascertain the availability of trademarks and trade names; registration with federal, state, and/or foreign agencies; and litigation at the administrative agency level (U.S. Patent and Trademark Office) and in the courts that involves trademark opposition or infringement matters.

The responsibilities of a paralegal who specializes in intellectual property law include:

- Conducting patent and trademark searches using computerized legal databases, online services, and the Internet;
- Preparing patent and/or trademark status summary reports;
- Drafting trademark and copyright registration applications;
- Maintaining a calendar of due dates for renewals, responses, and oppositions and for payment of patent annuities in foreign countries;
- Performing legal research regarding unfair competition;
- Assisting in opposition, interference, and infringement proceedings;
- Acting as liaison with foreign trademark/patent attorneys and agents; and
- Drafting license agreements regarding proprietary information and technology.

After receiving her bachelor's degree in psychology and business from UCLA in 1987, Tracy Bodovitz went to work for a Newport Beach, California, law firm that was willing to train her to work exclusively on trademark cases. After two years, one of the firm's clients, a southern

California swimwear manufacturer, offered Tracy a job. As director of international licensing, she coordinated trademark registrations with foreign law firms throughout the world. In addition, she worked in the area of licensing, which she believes offers unlimited opportunities for growth.

"Even if a paralegal works for a company that only sells their products domestically, they still need to register their trademarks overseas in order to avoid the possibility of trademark piracy, particularly in the South American countries," says Tracy. "Even in a domestic company, a trademark paralegal would gain valuable international experience."

Intellectual Property—Career Summary

Characteristics: Cases involve patent, trademark, copyright, and trade secrets law; transactional aspects involve searches and registrations, while court-related tasks involve infringement cases; highly specialized, technical area; technical undergraduate degree a plus; most opportunities in law firms.

Advantages: Specialization area; high salary potential; interesting work.

Disadvantages: Small job market; excellent credentials required; difficult to obtain jobs in corporations.

COMPUTERIZED LITIGATION SUPPORT

During the past decade, a new litigation subspecialty has emerged to provide an answer to the problem of document management for cases of all sizes and, in the process, has opened up new job opportunities for paralegals interested in computers. As you'll read in Chapter 6, computerized litigation support systems manage, access, and retrieve information and documents in a fraction of the time required by manual systems. Computerized systems are particularly efficient during discovery, when thousands of documents may need to be organized, indexed, and coded for retrieval at a moment's notice. For instance, an attorney might want a list of all of the references to a client occurring in documents dated from 1992 through 1995. As a paralegal, your task would be to search through all documents received from both your client and from the opposing counsel.

In the days before computers, you would have done the search manually—what a nightmare! Now you can see why so many paralegals burned out on litigation and eventually left the paralegal field entirely.

Thank goodness for computers. Today, this task becomes infinitely easier with the help of powerful personal computers, litigation support software, databases, optical scanners, and imaging equipment. As documents are received, they're scanned into databases on personal computers and coded according to predetermined categories for easy access and retrieval. Today, there are dozens of products available for litigation support. These and other applications of computers to the practice of law will be discussed in more detail in Chapter 6.

In computerized litigation support, a paralegal's responsibilities might include:

- Analyzing and selecting the hardware and software components of the computer system;
- Acting as liaison between the attorney and the computer programmer;
- Acting as project manager (which includes supervising other paralegals, scheduling timetables, and coordinating assignments);
- Acting as systems manager (which includes supervising backup and maintenance procedures);
- Training other support staff in the use of the system;
- Analyzing key issues and facts in the case in order to create the initial database; and
- Creating proprietary software programs if off-the-shelf programs are too expensive.

Keep in mind that many of the tasks listed above are done by paralegals with some experience. As an entry-level paralegal working in computerized litigation, your responsibilities might be limited to the more routine coding and input of documents.

Chyllene Cattie, a paralegal at a Philadelphia law firm, describes her responsibilities in this area: "A partner will tell me that he needs a database to do this or that. It's up to me to figure out how to do those things. I sit down with a computer programmer, figure out the needs of the attorney, and help design the program by making it applicable to that particular case. I hire temporary paralegals, usually graduates of local paralegal programs, to perform data entry. They extract information from documents that correlates to the specific fields in the software program that we have identified as important and relevant to the issues in the case. I'm also responsible for generating various reports from the system once it's designed."

Computerized Litigation Support —Career Summary

Characteristics: Court-related subspecialty of litigation; document intensive; computer skills a must; most jobs in law firms primarily on larger cases where systems are most cost effective.

Advantages: Fast-growing specialty area; high salary potential with experience; good foundation for careers in computers.

Disadvantages: Entry-level positions may involve tedious coding tasks; fewer opportunities in smaller law firms without the resources to purchase costly systems.

LABOR AND EMPLOYMENT LAW

In 1991, the nation watched as Clarence Thomas denied charges of sexual harassment brought by Anita Hill, a former employee. Although the most publicized of such charges, they are hardly the only ones. Issues involving sexual harassment, as well as job discrimination and union grievances, are in the news on a daily basis. In response to these issues, new laws are being passed. This has provided growing opportunities for lawyers and paralegals specializing in employment and labor law.

A labor law practice involves many different types of transactions, including collective bargaining, proceedings before the National Labor Relations Board (NLRB), arbitration, matters arising under federal and state wage and hour laws, Equal Employment Opportunity Commission (EEOC) investigations, discrimination cases, international labor matters, and litigation. The specific duties of a labor paralegal depend on whether he or she works in a law firm or a corporation and who the client is (a union, an employee, or management). Obviously, good people skills are needed in this specialty. Paralegals often must deal with sensitive issues, such as representing management in an employee discrimination case.

A paralegal who works for a labor law practice would be responsible for:

- Collecting and analyzing data for collective bargaining negotiations;
- Performing economic analyses of union proposals;

- Preparing comparisons of labor/management settlements from similar industries and analyzing recent trends;
- Attending bargaining sessions and taking notes;
- Preparing first drafts of bargaining agreements;
- Preparing for NLRB hearings;
- Drafting petition letters to the NLRB in defense of an unfair labor practice charge;
- Preparing for trial (similar to civil litigation) when formal complaints are issued by the NLRB;
- Preparing for arbitration proceedings;
- Reviewing and analyzing documents that relate to complaints of noncompliance to minimum wage or overtime provisions of federal or state laws;
- Preparing for EEOC investigations;
- Reviewing and analyzing employers' affirmative action plans; and
- Preparing documents in EEOC litigation matters.

Labor and Employment Law—Career Summary

Characteristics: Court-related tasks involving administrative and regulatory government agencies; cases involve discrimination, sexual harassment, union grievances; people skills a plus.

Advantages: Interesting work; good foundation for careers in human resources and labor relations.

Disadvantage: Emotional considerations working with certain issues.

EMPLOYEE BENEFITS

Employee benefits, which is also known as pension work, is an excellent specialty area for paralegals, given the growing number of regulations governing this area as well as the population trends toward aging and retirement.

The Employment Retirement Income Security Act of 1974 (ERISA) created new regulations to govern the qualification, disclosure, and reporting requirements of employee pension plans. In recent years, attorneys have turned more and more to paralegals to administer these regulations.

Paralegals should be familiar with several different types of employee benefit plans, including individual retirement accounts (IRAs), 401Ks, Keoghs, profit-sharing, money purchase, deferred compensation, stock bonus, employee stock purchase, and stock option plans. Pension and profit-sharing plans may be either qualified, which allows an employer deduction and requires IRS approval, or unqualified, which does not require IRS approval and grants no deduction to the employer.

Paralegals who specialize in employee benefit plans would be responsible for:

- Drafting plans and reviewing existing plans;

- Obtaining IRS approval of plans;

- Filing applications for IRS determination letters;

- Drafting plan summary descriptions;

- Assisting in the preparation of reports and disclosure information, including annual reports to the IRS and summary plan descriptions to plan participants;

- Drafting notification of participation, election to participate, beneficiary designation, and other election documents;

- Drafting promissory notes and salary assignments for participant loans;

- Answering employee inquiries (if working in a corporate setting);

- Determining valuation adjustments and making allocations to participants' accounts;

- Calculating participants' years of service for vesting purposes; and

- Administering plans, including paying termination benefits and loan proceeds, tracking loan repayments, and filing IRS 1099 forms for payments made.

One of the advantages of specializing in ERISA is that paralegals can easily transfer their skills to nonparalegal jobs in personnel or employee benefits departments. I know of one major San Francisco law firm that recently created a new title for ERISA paralegals—benefit specialist—that enables them to be paid more.

> ### *Employee Benefits:*
> ### *Employee Retirement Income Security Act (ERISA)—*
> ### *Career Summary*
>
> *Characteristics:* Transactional area involving pension plan work; requires a high level of responsibility; no court-related tasks.
>
> *Advantages:* Good foundation for careers in human resources; high salary potential.
>
> *Disadvantage:* Small job market.

ENVIRONMENTAL LAW

The decade of the nineties has been described as the green decade (in contrast to the greed decade of the 1980s); environmental and ecological issues are high priorities. A day doesn't go by when there isn't some environmental issue in the news. Environmental law has become a cash cow for law firms and is one of the fastest-growing specialty areas today.

Since the National Environmental Policy Act of 1970 became law, dozens of regulations and statutes have been created, sometimes making environmental law practice a regulatory nightmare. Cases can involve anything from compliance issues, such as obtaining permits under the Clean Water Act, to hazardous waste litigation, such as the asbestos cases that have been in the courts for years.

When preparing for proceedings before the U.S. Environmental Protection Agency (EPA) or similar state environmental agencies, environmental paralegals often perform tasks similar to those working in litigation. These tasks include document organization and analysis, identifying issues, organizing the witness file, drafting discovery documents, legal research and writing, scientific and technical research and writing, and exhibit and trial book preparation.

There are other responsibilities unique to environmental law, such as monitoring the rule-making activities of the EPA. In this regard, a paralegal would monitor the daily *Federal Register* for notices, proposals, and final rules that might affect a client. If a rule appears as if it might impact a client's interest, the paralegal may get involved in the rule-making process by helping to prepare and submit comments and alternative proposed language into the administrative record.

Environmental paralegals also attend and participate in administrative hearings and meetings. Some of their responsibilities might include studying the administrative record, drafting testimony for a company's representatives to present at hearing, and monitoring the proceedings of the hearing.

A large part of environmental law focuses on Superfund cases, which involve the remediation of hazardous waste sites. In 1980, the U.S. Congress enacted statutes to regulate the cleanup of contaminated sites and to create a "superfund" of $1.5 billion to fund the remediation.

Under the federal Superfund law, generators of hazardous wastes are liable for completing a cleanup even if the site has been abandoned. These complex cases can be extremely interesting to work on, but they can be disturbing as well. (In environmental law, sometimes the more you know, the more you wish you didn't.) In a Superfund case, a paralegal's responsibility often begins when a company is notified of its potential liability. Some specific tasks include:

- Investigating why a client has been named a potentially responsible party (PRP);
- Filing a request for the information the EPA used to identify the client's connection to the site;
- Assisting in drafting responses to the EPA's request, which involves examining the manifests, logs, and reports, as well as interviewing personnel;
- Attending Steering Committee meetings with other PRPs in order to better facilitate negotiations and settlements with the EPA;
- Implementing a computerized document management and retrieval database in order to organize and monitor documents received from the EPA, the client, and other PRPs;
- Researching and monitoring changes in state and federal legislation and administrative regulations; and
- Preparing a "waste-in" summary, i.e., a detailed analysis of who sent what waste and in what amounts to the site.

Kim Marshall, a former paralegal at a Detroit, Michigan, law firm, specialized in environmental law. She worked exclusively on Superfund cases and handled thirty-five Superfund sites that involved a tremendous amount of documentation and analysis. In addition, she did a lot of substantive work, including drafting affidavits, interrogatories, and deposition questions, as well as attending meetings. One of the things she enjoyed most about her job was working on multiple cases simultaneously.

She advises anyone considering a paralegal career in environmental law to be highly organized so that you can manage large quantities of documents, and to be flexible so that you can take on responsibility at a moment's notice. You need to be ready to take the ball and run with it.

According to Kim, other qualities necessary to succeed in this area include analytical skills to understand Superfund proceedings, strong research skills to monitor changing legislation, and the ability to communicate with the agencies, clients, and other parties involved.

Environmental Law—Career Summary

Characteristics: Court-related tasks involving government regulatory and compliance issues as well as toxic waste tort litigation; critical-thinking and problem-analysis skills are important, as is familiarity with technical terminology; majority of jobs are in law firms.

Advantages: Fast-growing specialty; interesting, relevant issues; high salary potential.

Disadvantage: Small job market.

BANKRUPTCY

There was a time when working in bankruptcy law was considered the bottom of the barrel. Not anymore. The number of bankruptcy petitions filed over the past decade has more than doubled, from 364,000 petitions filed in 1985, to 845,000 filed in 1994. Despite the upswing in the economy in the past few years, bankruptcy is still big business. Companies are still downsizing and reorganizing, which creates continued opportunities for paralegals in this area.

Bankruptcy is the legal process that, under federal law, gives a debtor a fresh start and ensures that his or her creditors are treated as fairly as possible. There are several forms of relief available under the federal bankruptcy laws. Those most commonly used are Chapter 7, which involves liquidating a person's assets; Chapter 11, which involves reorganizing a corporation; and Chapter 13, which involves adjusting a person's debts. To initiate bankruptcy proceedings, either a voluntary petition or an involuntary petition must be filed by the debtor or creditor, respectively, in bankruptcy court. Law firms that specialize in bankruptcy may act as a trustee or represent the debtor or the creditor in court proceedings.

Working for a debtor. No matter what chapter a bankruptcy case comes under, all cases begin with the filing of the debtor's Petition for Relief. At a firm that represents a debtor, a paralegal's duties begin with the preparation of the schedules and financial statements that accompany this petition. The paralegal aids in the disclosure of information to interested parties about the debtor's financial situation; ensures that the debtor fulfills his or her obligations to creditors, the court, and the bankruptcy trustee; and, to the degree possible, preserves the debtor's assets. Some of the assignments would include:

- Gathering information and facts about the client's financial position;
- Drafting the bankruptcy petition;
- Arranging for UCC and real property searches;
- Preparing a schedule of the debtor's assets and liabilities;
- Listing claims for any property exempt under the bankruptcy code;
- Preparing a statement of affairs;
- Preparing for the first meeting of creditors;
- Drafting and filing the debtor's monthly financial statements (in Chapter 11 cases);
- Drafting complaints in adversary proceedings; and
- Attending Chapter 13 plan confirmation hearings.

Working for a creditor. The primary responsibility of a lawyer who represents a creditor is to protect and preserve the creditor's interests and obtain payment of his or her claim. Paralegals on this side of a bankruptcy case would be responsible for managing information and documents using litigation support software, analyzing financial reports, drafting complaints, motions and other pleadings, legal and factual research, acting as client liaison, assisting in bankruptcy hearings, and attending Section 341 creditors' meetings.

Working for a trustee. Bankruptcy paralegals may be employed by lawyers or nonlawyers who act as the bankruptcy trustee. Once a bankruptcy is filed, the trustee is responsible for the recovery and liquidation of the debtor's assets and the payment of creditors' claims. Some of the paralegal's responsibilities include:

- Preparing demand letters to institutions and companies to notify them of the bankruptcy and request that they turn any of the debtor's funds over to the trustee;

- Arranging for the appraisal of the debtor's assets;

- Monitoring any transfer of assets or expenditure of funds during the bankruptcy proceedings;

- Arranging for notice in newspapers concerning the sale of the debtor's property;

- Preparing a full accounting of the property sold; and

- Reviewing all claims before distribution of funds to creditors.

Career Tip

It is important to understand that, similar to probate but unlike litigation, the process of bankruptcy and foreclosures can be handled by the paralegal from beginning to end. This is due to the fact that the documentation involved is routine, predictable, and ordered.

Kim Morzak worked as a bankruptcy paralegal for a large Dallas law firm where most of her work involved Chapter 11 corporate reorganizations. When working on Chapter 11 cases, she says it's helpful to have a good understanding of financial statements. Since bankruptcy is extremely document intensive, you need excellent organizational skills. In some cases, she often received hundreds of proof of claim forms from creditors that must then be reconciled to the debtor's records. To assist in the number crunching, she used computer spreadsheet programs.

What Kim liked most about her job was the fact that the attorneys she worked for trusted her enough to give her substantive assignments. She had a great deal of client contact and did a lot of document drafting.

Kim's advice to entry-level paralegals is to do whatever it takes to get your foot in the door. In the beginning, you might not get the greatest assignments but you'll learn a lot, which will help you later on. Also, it's important to establish a good rapport with the people in the courts and various agencies you'll be dealing with because they can make life easier for you.

Mortgage foreclosures. Foreclosure work is a subspecialty of bankruptcy law and has proved quite lucrative for many law firms. Bankruptcy paralegals specializing in foreclosure work are employed in law firms, mortgage companies, banks, or government agencies on cases involving residential or commercial foreclosures. Some responsibilities in this area include:

- Collecting and reviewing lender's documents such as original note, deed of trust, title policy, payment history, principal balance, etc., in order to initiate action;
- Ordering current title evidence and updates, determining who must be given notice of foreclosure and preparing a list of parties entitled to notice;
- Ordering a bankruptcy search to ensure that foreclosure has not been prohibited by a bankruptcy court;
- Drafting foreclosure documents and delivering documents to the public trustee who will complete the notice mailings and arrange for all publications;
- Preparing the bid and delivering it to the public trustee prior to the sale;
- Attending the sale and/or following up on result of the sale; and
- Preparing the trustee's deed.

Laurie Roselle, paralegal manager for a New York City law firm, describes what she looks for in hiring bankruptcy paralegals: "He or she has got to be interested in financial matters, good at numbers, very meticulous, a good investigator, and a good people person." Given the court-related tasks in bankruptcy law, Laurie also looks for paralegals with litigation experience. And because bankruptcy proceedings place enormous financial and emotional burdens on the parties involved, paralegals who work in this area should be adept at handling sensitive personal issues.

> ### *Bankruptcy—Career Summary*
>
> *Characteristics:* Growing specialty due to a volatile economy; court-related tasks; investigative and people skills a plus; cases involve representation of debtor, creditor, or trustee; jobs primarily in law firms.
>
> *Advantages:* Specialization area; high salary potential; good freelance opportunities.
>
> *Disadvantages:* Small job market; emotional elements of work; job market cyclical depending on economic conditions.

IMMIGRATION LAW

Due to the continuing influx of immigrants into the United States and the trend toward more multinational companies, immigration work is on the rise. Opportunities range from working in a small law firm representing immigrants seeking legalization to working in a large law firm or corporation representing multinational companies in complex business immigration matters.

In both types of cases, attorneys are increasingly relying on paralegals to perform tasks such as:

- Performing the initial client interviews;
- Acting as the primary contact with government agencies such as the Department of Justice, the Immigration and Naturalization Service (INS), the Department of Labor (DOL), and the Department of State;
- Assisting corporate clients in obtaining temporary working visas and permanent residence;
- Preparing the client for INS interviews;
- Drafting applications and petitions for filing with the INS and DOL;
- Researching the availability of foreign documents and immigrant and nonimmigrant visa alternatives;
- Coordinating translation of foreign documents; and
- Drafting the application for alien employment certification.

Given the tremendous amount of client contact in this specialty area, a paralegal must possess excellent communication skills, such as interviewing and negotiating. Since paralegals oftentimes conduct the initial interview, being bilingual or multilingual would be helpful. In addition, a sensitivity to the client's anxieties about the process is also necessary. Paralegals working in immigration law often cite the fact that they perform complex and sophisticated tasks that in other practice areas would be handled by attorneys.

One immigration paralegal I spoke to at a large New York law firm confirmed this by stating, "Since immigration law is very administrative in nature, 90 percent of the work on routine business visas is done by paralegals. As a result, our international corporate clients get tremendous value for their money.

"There is more personal contact with clients in immigration work than most other legal specialties. Since paralegals are the primary contact, they often learn personal details about an individual's background that they wouldn't have learned working in litigation, for instance. You need to be sensitive to these issues because it is a very anxious time for them (the clients).

"The most satisfying thing is to take a case that doesn't look promising on paper and put together a whole package that ultimately convinces the immigration service to issue the visa."

Immigration Law—Career Summary

Characteristics: Transactional area involving work with federal administrative agencies; no court-related tasks; bilingual and people skills helpful; jobs available in law firms and government agencies; high degree of autonomy and responsibility.

Advantages: Psychological benefits of helping people obtain citizenship, permanent residence, visas; high salary potential if work for large immigration law firm with multinational corporate clients.

Disadvantages: Lower salary potential likely if working for a small firm with noncorporate clients; small job market.

Other Practice Areas

Besides the four traditional practice areas discussed in Chapter 3, as well as the fast-growing specialties detailed above, there are several other areas of paralegal employment you should be aware of, including:

- Family law

- Criminal law
- Workers' compensation
- Personal injury

The 1996 O. J. Simpson criminal trial and the custody hearing for his children have greatly increased the country's awareness of criminal and family law procedures. Family law cases deal with issues relating to divorce, custody, child support, and adoption. Both family and criminal law involve court-related tasks. Job opportunities in these areas can be found either in small law firms or government agencies. Large law firms generally do not handle these types of cases.

The major drawback to working in these areas, besides a limited job market, is the emotional stress that sometimes accompanies the work. Because of potential burnout, I believe that these are not particularly good areas for a long-term paralegal career. Despite this, I have spoken to a number of paralegals working in criminal and family law who wouldn't do anything else.

Paralegals working in family law might perform the following duties: collect background information on the client, complete domestic relations questionnaire, assist in preparing monthly income and expense reports, determine spousal and child support, analyze retirement benefits, draft pleadings (such as petitions, complaints, protective orders, stipulations, and settlement agreements), prepare for trial, and coordinate post-hearing follow-up, to name just a few.

Responsibilities in criminal law include preparing motion for bond reduction, arranging for bail, gathering information for plea bargaining, obtaining discovery (such as police reports and warrants), examining physical evidence, preparing for preliminary hearing, drafting pleadings, attending conferences, preparing sentencing information, and researching legal issues.

Workers' compensation is a specialty that involves the decisions, regulations, and rulings of administrative agencies. One such agency is the Workers' Compensation Appeals Board (WCAB), which regulates the compensation of people who are injured on the job. As with other administrative agencies, the WCAB allows nonlawyers, including paralegals, to represent clients before it. As a result, paralegals working in this field often have a wide range of responsibilities, some of which are similar to those of litigation paralegals.

Personal injury law. Personal injury cases involve the legal principles of negligence as they relate to the operation of motor vehicles. Due to the

79

medical nature of this specialty, law firms are beginning to hire paralegals who were formerly nurses. The term "nurse-paralegal" is popping up more and more in classified ads for these jobs. Some paralegal responsibilities in personal injury law include:

- Obtaining accident information during the initial client interview;
- Preparing a factual synopsis on liability and damages for each injured person;
- Obtaining a copy of the accident report and photographs of the accident scene;
- Contacting witnesses to obtain statements; and
- Preparing a draft of the settlement letter or complaint if filing suit.

Once a suit has been filed, paralegal tasks in these cases are similar to those in litigation during discovery and trial preparation. One of the differences is that in most accident cases the issues are relatively simple, and there are fewer defendants than in other types of litigation cases where there may be dozens of parties involved.

If you have a background in the medical field, personal injury law might be something you'll want to consider.

Career Tip

For nurses interested in working in law, either as a paralegal or consultant, contact the American Association of Legal Nurse Consultants (AALNC), 4700 West Lake Avenue, Glenview, Illinois 60025-1485, or call 847-375-4713. Founded in 1989, the AALNC is a nonprofit organization dedicated to the professional enhancement of registered nurses working in a consulting capacity in the legal field. Legal nurse consultants or nurse-paralegals offer attorneys support in medical issues involving personal injury, product liability, medical malpractice, toxic torts, workers' compensation, and criminal cases.

Now that you have a general idea of what paralegals do, you can combine this knowledge with your own individual interests, skills, and experience to help you with your job search.

So far, this book has looked at who paralegals are, where they work, and what they do. The next chapter examines another vital issue—how to become a paralegal—and addresses educational and training alternatives and the skills that are needed for a successful career.

CHAPTER 5

How Do You Become a Paralegal?

Skills, Education, and Training

The roots of education are bitter, but the fruit is sweet.
Aristotle

■

It's your first day on the job. You're a newly minted paralegal armed with a certificate from an ABA-approved paralegal program. You also have a bachelor's degree in something interesting, but not too practical, such as English literature or philosophy. An associate, looking ragged and hurried, calls you into her office, mutters something about a partnership agreement, and barks an assignment at you that sounds pretty vague and incomprehensible. You don't want to appear stupid and ask questions, so you sit there and nod as if you know exactly what she is talking about. It's over in about a minute and a half, but the experience leaves you feeling confused and panicky.

Lawyers are notorious for giving sketchy assignments and then disappearing for days, only to reappear 10 minutes before the assignment is due. Believe it or not, lawyers don't always know exactly what they want. You could be given an assignment that gets changed five times before they figure out what they're after! This chapter gives you insight into the kinds of skills, education, and formal training you'll need to help you to cope with these and other attorney foibles and to perform your job tasks with confidence.

Since the scenario mentioned above has occurred so often in my own experiences as a paralegal, I have come to identify two abilities that are essential to success in the field: (1) the ability to locate resources and (2) common sense. I can't stress enough how important these are, and I guarantee that you'll rely on them daily.

Being able to locate resources and access information is extremely crucial for paralegals—and for people in many other occupations—as we move toward the twenty-first century. Lawyers are always in a hurry and are always under pressure, and they generally want everything done yesterday. You need to know where to go for information if you're given a vague assignment and no one is available to answer your questions. The source could be a law library, a computer database file, the Internet, a state regulatory agency, or any of the hundreds of other sources of data that exist. The point is, oftentimes when you are given an assignment you will not know the answer. But you will be expected to know how and where to find it.

Common sense cannot be taught. You either have it or you don't. Strange as it may seem, most legal assignments require 10 percent ability and knowledge and 90 percent common sense.

SKILLS NEEDED TO SUCCEED

The skills you need for success with the day-to-day tasks and responsibilities of a paralegal can be broken down into three major groups:

- *Organizational skills.* The ability to stay on top of details; to manage, retrieve, and organize documents; and to administer, coordinate, and schedule.

- *Communication skills.* The ability to get ideas across verbally and in writing (including legal writing, interpersonal relations, negotiating, investigating, interviewing, and supervising).

- *Analytical skills.* The ability to conduct legal, factual, statistical, and legislative research; to reason; to extract and utilize information; to interpret and apply laws and regulations; and to analyze and summarize facts and documents.

Most tasks performed by paralegals use all of these skill groups in some combination. For instance, I was once given an assignment to analyze and evaluate the defendants' responses to all of the plaintiff's requests for the production of documents and interrogatories to make sure that the defendants had, in fact, produced all of the documents they said that they had. I was also asked to make recommendations about additional documents to request from the defendants based upon my knowledge of the case.

Successful completion of the assignment depended on using each of the three skill areas in the following manner: organizational—locating and retrieving specific documents; analytical—extracting and interpreting information in the defendants' responses in relation to what was requested; and communication—writing a detailed memorandum to the partner on the case.

Writing Skills

If I had to choose one particular skill as the most important, it would be writing. Not legal writing, mind you, just plain old writing. What's the difference? The first is meant to intimidate you. The second is meant to enlighten you.

One of the reasons people are so put off by lawyers is legalese—the language they use. Legal writing is often filled with confusing (some would say unnecessary, redundant, vague, and meaningless) words and phrases.

"Good legal writing should not differ, without good reason, from ordinary, well-written English," says Richard Wydick, law school professor at the University of California, Davis. Professor Wydick's book, *Plain English for Lawyers*, is one of the bestselling books ever written for the field. It was instrumental in promoting what is known as the "plain-language" movement in law that began in the mid-1970s.

Plain English for Lawyers contains the following chapters, the titles of which offer sound advice about good writing: "Omit Surplus Words," "Use Base Verbs, Not Nominalizations," "Prefer the Active Voice," "Use Short Sentences," "Arrange Your Words with Care," "Use Familiar, Concrete Words," and "Avoid Language Quirks."

Career Tip

Remember that writing is the meat and potatoes of most paralegal assignments. If you like to write, this is a viable career option. One of the first things I learned as a paralegal is to put everything in writing, no matter how small or seemingly insignificant. In fact, a "memorandum to file" probably is a paralegal's best friend. The reason? Three years from now, when you're no longer working on the case, someone else may have to reconstruct it from your memoranda. The more clearly you document the things in it, the easier it will be to reconstruct. (Incidentally, memos to file are also great for proving that you actually performed a specific task as requested.)

Technology and Computer Skills

I cannot emphasize enough how important using technology and computers will be in your paralegal career. I use the term technology because it represents the use of a broader skill set needed for interacting with software programs, hardware, operating systems, networks, e-mail, imaging technology, the Internet, and so on.

Since writing the first edition of this book in the spring of 1989 and the second edition in the spring of 1993, the use of technology in law firms and employers' expectations of paralegals using them has skyrocketed. It is no longer enough to just know word processing. Specific computer skills will be discussed further in Chapter 6.

Checklist of Skills

Based on my personal experiences, the following is a summary of the different types of skills you'll need to succeed as a paralegal. They are not in any particular order. Review each one honestly in terms of your own abilities and interests. This will help you in determining whether a paralegal career is right for you.

- Writing skills
- Technology and computer skills
- Verbal communication
- Research skills
- Ability to work on many assignments at once
- Ability to work independently with little supervision
- Ability to prioritize
- Analytical ability
- Investigative ability
- Attention to detail
- Organizational ability
- Problem-solving ability

Of these skills, prioritizing assignments without panicking and working with minimal supervision are elemental to on-the-job success. Working at a law firm requires handling many different cases and clients at once. For example, you're in the middle of drafting a legal research memorandum for one attorney—due the next day—when suddenly another attorney rushes into your office and hands you an assignment that needs to be done before the end of the day. Next, a client calls and asks you to send out the stock certificates that you promised would be ready three days ago. And then, almost at the same moment, your paralegal supervisor phones to ask for your help on a rush project for the real estate department. You must be able to determine the relative importance of each of these assignments and the most efficient and effective order for carrying them out.

This scenario is more likely to occur in a law firm than in a corporate legal department. As was discussed in Chapter 2, paralegals in a corporate legal department work for one client—the corporation—so there are usually fewer fires to put out than at a law firm, where multiple clients generally want things done now. Prioritizing is essential.

Regarding supervision, attorneys are usually too busy to hover over you and monitor everything you do. This is great once you're experienced and know what you're doing, but it can be a bit nerve-racking for new paralegals who may have no clue about how to proceed on their own. Be patient—you may find the opportunity to work independently one of the pluses of the career.

EDUCATION AND TRAINING

Because standardized educational requirements have not been accepted by the profession industrywide and because employers use their own criteria when hiring paralegals, entry into the field is open to people with a wide range of educational backgrounds and experience. Although it is possible to land a position that provides on-the-job training or to become a paralegal via promotion, current trends indicate that people with some formal education or training—a bachelor's degree, a paralegal certificate, or an associate degree in paralegal studies—tend to be hired.

The Evolution of Paralegal Education

Before the various types of paralegal programs available today are discussed, a brief look at the history of paralegal education and training will help give you some perspective.

Education and training for paralegals have evolved steadily over the last thirty years. Before formal programs were established in the early 1970s, most training took place on the job. The advent of certificate-granting programs signaled the growing acceptance within the legal profession of paralegal as a new career niche. And in 1972, the career gained further legitimacy when the ABA's Special Committee on Lay

Educational Background of Paralegals*

At least 30 college hours—14%
Associate degree—21%
Bachelor's degree—54%
Graduate degree—5%
Ph.D. or J.D.—less than 1%
Paralegal training in addition to college—59%
Paralegal training as part of college curriculum—25%
ABA-approved program—64% (up from 52% in 1992)
CLA designation—16%

Responses may include more than one answer

Source: 1995 *Paralegal Compensation and Benefits Report,* National Federation of Paralegal Associations, Inc.

Assistants developed guidelines to evaluate and thus accredit paralegal training programs. The number of formal training programs nationwide grew from a few dozen to several hundred between 1972 and 1977.

Despite the proliferation of these programs, paralegals, as such, were still relatively unknown to many prospective employers. The 1970s saw most paralegal functions performed by legal secretaries and people trained in other fields.

Therese Cannon, former dean of the School of Paralegal Studies at the University of West Los Angeles, recalls the emergence of the paralegal profession. "When I started out as placement director in 1974, almost no one in Los Angeles knew what a paralegal was. There were almost no jobs for paralegals. Almost all of the lawyers who contacted the school wanted a smart legal secretary who could operate independently. For the next six or seven years we had to do a tremendous amount of promotional work. Both UCLA and our school were instrumental in building the paralegal field here. It all changed around 1980, and in the next five years the number of job openings in Los Angeles had expanded dramatically."

By the mid-1980s, employers had begun to recognize formal paralegal education as a measure of competence in the field. Over 85 percent of the paralegals who responded to the National Federation of Paralegal Associations (NFPA) 1995 *Paralegal Compensation and Benefits Report* indicated that they had received formal training; that compares with 30 percent who in a 1982 survey said they had had formal training. Today, it is difficult to obtain paralegal employment without a paralegal certificate, a bachelor's degree, or both.

Formal Programs

Today, over 35,000 students are enrolled in approximately 800 institutions nationwide that provide formal paralegal training. This compares to 600 programs in 1993. These institutions include two-year colleges, four-year universities and colleges, technical schools, and proprietary schools, and their programs may lead to a certificate, the associate degree, or the bachelor's degree.

Certificate programs. Certificate programs are the most prevalent type of paralegal training and are offered by two- and four-year colleges, technical schools, and proprietary schools. For the most part, these programs provide only legal training although some do include general education courses. They can take anywhere from three months (if attended full-time) to over two years to complete and are recommended for individuals who possess a bachelor's degree, have completed 30 to 60 units of college credit, or have some work experience.

Career Tip

I've noticed an increasing number of people attracted to a paralegal career because they are under the assumption that they can complete a certificate in three to six months. While some three-month programs do exist, the majority of certificate programs take an average of 1½ to 2 years to complete. The trend in paralegal education is to require more courses, not less.

To some, the major drawback of the shorter certificate programs is that they provide only a cursory pass of the material—their short time frame makes it impossible to cover subjects in detail. Lyla Hines, formerly a paralegal program instructor in Dallas, observes, "I think that in some instances they try to shove too much information into the students without sufficient background. I understand the desire to have successful programs, but you can't take someone who has no legal background and expect them to learn torts and contracts as well as the practical aspects of working in a law office, all in a 30-hour course."

The following are examples of the curricula of two certificate programs; the first is ABA approved, and the second is not.

St. Mary's College in Moraga, California, began its paralegal program in 1977 and received ABA approval in 1978. Applicants must have completed at least 30 semester units of academic credit with a grade of C or better. Most courses in the program may be applied to a B.A. degree.

Graduates receive a paralegal certificate and can complete the certificate in one year or four quarters. Students must take twelve courses (seven required and five electives) and can specialize in litigation, corporate/business, or probate. The required courses are:

Contract Law
Corporate Law I
Legal Concepts
Legal Research and Writing
Litigation I
Litigation II (Discovery)
Real Estate Law

The five elective courses can be taken from a number of areas, including administrative, bankruptcy, environmental, criminal, family, immigration, intellectual property, probate, tax, personal injury, computers, estate planning, workers' compensation, and dispute resolution.

Career Tip

Generally, certificate programs aren't recommended for recent high school graduates who have had little or no professional work experience. For people who have experience in the workforce and want to change careers, however, these programs are ideal.

The second example is the curriculum from the Attorney Assistant Program of Sonoma State University, part of the California State University System. Requirements for entrance include either an A.A. degree, *or* at least 56 college-level semester units, *or* at least five years of legal experience. The certificate requires 30 program units, including 20 units of required courses and 10 units of electives. The required courses are:

Introduction to law
Legal research
Legal writing
Civil procedure: pleadings
Civil procedure: discovery
Legal ethics
Internship: job search
Internship: work experience

Three- and two-unit electives include business organizations, family law, personal injury litigation, probate, real property, workers' compensation, criminal law, administrative hearing procedure, estate planning, evidence code, drafting contracts, juvenile law, California corporations, law practice management, computer use in law, and land use/environmental law.

One-unit electives include interviewing and investigation, judicial arbitration, landlord-tenant law, labor law and wrongful termination, construction law, medical records review, efficient document management, how to operate a successful freelance paralegal business, liability insurance coverage in litigation, law office management, and discovery management.

One of the interesting aspects about this program is that, unlike most educational programs, it is run by a former paralegal, not an attorney or an educator. This is clearly evident in some of the more practical 1-unit electives listed above.

Associate degree programs. Some community and junior colleges and four-year universities and colleges offer two-year associate degrees in paralegal studies. Admission requirements for these programs include a high school diploma, and, possibly, college-level aptitude test scores, writing samples, letters of recommendation, and personal interviews.

The curriculum usually is a combination of general education requirements, core legal courses (in research, writing, and law office management and an introduction to the field), business law, civil procedure, and legal specialty courses.

Cañada College in Redwood City, California, offers both a 27-unit certificate program and a 60-unit Associate in Science degree. The associate degree program includes the 27 units of the certificate program plus 20 units in general education (including a physical education class) as well as 13 units of electives. Within the 27-unit certificate core, required courses include:

Introduction to the legal system
Legal research and writing
Civil litigation and trial preparation
Paralegalism and the study of legal ethics

Electives include torts, estate administration, family law, corporations and business entities, real property law, bankruptcy and debt collection, advanced civil litigation, advanced legal research and writing, contracts, cooperative education, independent study, selected topics, and microcomputer applications.

Career Tip

These programs are recommended for high school graduates with little or no professional work experience. An associate degree in paralegal studies can be used to land a job as a paralegal or as credit toward obtaining a bachelor's degree. (Being able to go on for a four-year degree at some later point is the major benefit and attraction of an associate degree.)

Bachelor's degree programs. A growing number of universities and colleges offer majors or minors in paralegal studies in their four-year degree programs. Although many of these were initiated in the early to mid-1970s, they are not as well known for their paralegal training as are the certificate programs.

Based on current hiring trends, The National Federation of Paralegal Associations, Inc. (NFPA) is now recommending that future paralegals should have a four-year degree to enter the profession.

The curriculum requirements of these programs usually include general education and business courses as well as legal specialty courses. The programs combine both a generalist's and a specialist's approach to the paralegal field. Many also offer internships in the senior year, which provide students with the opportunity to integrate classroom learning and on-the-job experience.

Jill E. Martin, attorney, professor, and chair of the Department of Legal Studies at Connecticut's Quinnipiac College, suggests that four-year programs provide recent high school graduates with the opportunity to attain the maturity needed for a job as a paralegal in a law firm, particularly when the program includes an internship and courses in law office management. She believes that certificate programs may be more suitable for older students who have had some college and work experience. With the trend toward more rather than less education, Jill believes that four-year programs are the wave of the future.

Quinnipiac's legal studies major is not a prelaw program. Students receive a Bachelor of Arts in legal studies, which is approved by the American Bar Association. The curriculum consists of a combination of liberal arts and business courses and thirteen legal studies courses. The following legal studies courses were required in the 1996–1997 school year: proseminar (introduction to the paralegal career), introduction to the American legal system, library methods in the law, civil procedure I, civil procedure II, legal writing, law office management, legal internship I, and legal internship II. Electives could be chosen from criminal justice; business entities; administrative agencies; law and older persons; family law; constitution and the courts; wills, probate, and estate administration; and land transfer and closing procedures.

Career Tip

A bachelor's degree program is recommended for high school graduates who are planning to obtain a degree from a four-year college. The major benefit of a bachelor's degree program is that it provides the student with a liberal arts background and skills that are immediately transferable to the workplace. Also, since the programs take four years to complete, each subject can be covered in depth. For instance, a legal writing and research course in a four-year program may take two semesters to complete, while the same material in a three-month certificate program may be covered in one month or less.

Master's programs. Master degree programs in paralegal studies are a relatively new phenomena. They might be suited for career paralegals wishing to advance into legal-related areas such as law office management, as well as individuals who had to put off law school but still have a strong interest in the law. The following master's degrees are offered:

Master of Arts in Legal Studies

The University of Illinois at Springfield
Springfield, Illinois
217-786-6535

Montclair State University
Upper Montclair, New Jersey
201-655-4152

Webster University
St. Louis, Missouri
314-968-7432

Duke University, School of Law
Durham, North Carolina
919-613-7200

Master of Arts in Legal Administration

> Marymount University
> Arlington, Virginia
> 703-284-5910

Master of Science in Justice and Public Safety

> Auburn University at Montgomery
> Montgomery, Alabama
> 334-244-3697

Home study programs. You may have seen the ads for home study programs on television. Thanks in part to the recession of the early 1990s, these correspondence courses are doing a good business. My personal advice would be to stay away from them if at all possible. Home study is okay for some fields, but this is not one of them. Besides, you will be competing with too many people who have attended traditional educational institutions, which are generally considered to be superior to home study. You don't need to give an employer an excuse to toss your resume into the reject pile!

Career Tip

If you are still interested in this option, however, you might want to contact the Distance Education and Training Council, which is an accrediting agency authorized by the U.S. Department of Education to evaluate home study programs. Their address is 1601 18th Street, NW, Washington, D.C. 20009; telephone: 202-234-5100.

No matter what option you choose, I recommend two sources for information on paralegal programs in the United States:

National Federation of Paralegal Associations, Inc. offers a directory of paralegal education programs for $15. The directory lists over 770 paralegal programs and includes information on how to choose a program. You can also find a list of programs by state through its Web page at www.paralegals.org. There you will also find out how to get its free brochure called "How to Choose a Paralegal Education Program."

You can purchase the American Bar Association's *Guide for Legal Assistant Education Programs* for $7.50 by contacting the ABA's service center at 312-988-5522. The booklet lists over 210 ABA-approved paralegal programs.

Making a Choice

As you have seen, there are several kinds of formal paralegal training programs available today. Paralegal education is big business, and new schools are opening their doors every day. Listed below are things you should consider when deciding on the program that is best for you.

ABA approval. ABA approval is voluntary on the part of the institution. But for many employers, an ABA-approved program signifies quality. Out of the over 770 formal programs that operate today, approximately 210, or only 27 percent, are ABA approved. Earning approval means a program meets strict guidelines adopted by the ABA's Standing Committee on Legal Assistants regarding the number of semester hours and types of courses required for certification or a degree. The approval process also includes a review of a school's faculty, admission requirements, administrative staff, and job placement service.

Admission requirements. Admission requirements vary widely and depend on the type of certification that's offered. A certificate program generally requires either a bachelor's degree or work experience and/or one to two years of college. Programs that offer either a two-year or a four-year degree require a high school diploma and may also require work experience, aptitude or achievement test scores, and demonstrated writing ability.

Length of study. The length of time required to complete a paralegal training or education program varies from three months to four years, depending on the type. (Keep in mind that most three-month programs require a bachelor's degree for admission.) Many programs offer full-time and part-time options with both day and evening classes.

Curricula. Most programs use a combination of two basic curriculum models—general, broad-based legal training and intensified training in legal specialty areas. General legal courses usually include an introduction to the paralegal profession, civil procedure, criminal law, legal research and writing, law office management, and, possibly, computer literacy. Legal specialty courses include real estate, probate, corporate/business, tax, criminal, and family law; estate planning; and litigation. All programs should offer courses in theory as well as practical skills.

Career Tip

There is one thing to keep in mind regarding ABA approval. Just because a program is not ABA approved does not mean it isn't of good quality. I've been told by some program administrators that receiving ABA approval is quite expensive. Some programs cannot afford this cost, which includes paying the ABA-approval team's travel and lodging to the school in order to qualify the program.

Faculty composition. The qualifications of the people teaching the course work are just as important as the material that is covered. Instructors are usually attorneys, working paralegals, business executives, and specialists with expertise in a particular field (such as computers). The selection of instructors depends on factors such as teaching ability, work experience, expertise, and experience with paralegals in the workplace.

Placement services. Reputable programs provide job placement services for current students and alumni. These services should include opportunities for internships. (As Chapter 7 reveals, internships are a great way to obtain your first paralegal position while learning valuable on-the-job skills.)

Computer facilities. Due to the increased demand for computer-literate paralegals, most programs today offer computer training courses. A publication called *Core Competencies for Paralegal Programs* by the American Association for Paralegal Education (AAfPE) suggests that quality paralegal programs teach students how to use on-line and CD-ROM–based legal research products, such as LEXIS and WESTLAW, as well as at least one commonly used word processing program, database program, and spreadsheet program.

If you are enrolled in one of the few programs that do not offer computer classes, other resources for obtaining computer skills include community education programs sponsored by your local community, general computer classes at local community colleges, and self-study programs if you have your own computer at home. However, these sources will not introduce you to computer applications in the law.

The message here is: Computer training is now a necessary part of paralegal education.

Enrollment. Class size generally should not exceed thirty-five students. Remember, the smaller the class, the more individual attention you'll receive and the better the student participation and interaction.

Career Tip

Some words of warning: Ever since the U.S. Department of Labor released statistics on the paralegal profession in 1987, a whole new crop of proprietary paralegal programs and schools have sprung up. Some are good, others aren't. Be wary of the ones that are not ABA approved, charge a lot of money, and promise that you'll make $40,000 to start as an entry-level paralegal. Some of these programs are just cashing in on the federal statistics and have targeted paralegal education mainly as a way to fatten their wallets. Be a cautious consumer and get the facts before you invest your time and money in what could be a less than reputable program.

Cost. When looking for the program that's right for you, don't be fooled by the notion that the more one costs, the better it is—that's not always true. Costs vary widely. One of the major factors seems to be whether or not you attend a public or private institution. Costs can range anywhere from several hundred dollars to over $6,000, which is about what several private San Francisco Bay Area universities now charge.

As I mentioned earlier in this chapter, NFPA has a brochure called *How To Choose a Paralegal Education Program.* It is available for free through its Web page at www.paralegals.org. This pamphlet was put together in association with the American Bar Association (ABA), American Association for Paralegal Education (AAfPE), Association of Legal Administrators (ALA), National Association of Legal Assistants (NALA) and the Legal Assistant Management Association (LAMA).

Additional criteria listed in the brochure for evaluating a program include education objectives, reputation, membership in AAfPE, qualifications of the program administrator, inclusion of experimental education, and student services.

Look hard at what a particular school offers and what it costs; then compare that school to some others. Before you decide on a particular program, it's important to evaluate not only the program itself but your own situation. Are you a high school graduate with no experience? Are you returning to the workforce after raising a family? Do you want to change careers? Do you have the time to pursue a program for two or three years? The paralegal field is open to a wide variety of individuals with different educational and work backgrounds, and there are many different programs available. Pick and choose carefully.

Laurie Roselle, paralegal coordinator at a large law firm in New York City, has some sound advice: "Don't jump into a program. Don't take the word of the program director that the school is the best thing since sliced bread, because, of course, that's what they are all going to say. Talk to former students. Call paralegal associations. Conduct your own research."

Do you really need that piece of paper? Only 15 percent of the paralegals who responded to the NFPA's 1995 *Paralegal Compensation and Benefits Report* had no formal training, down from 28 percent in 1988. The availability of paralegal training programs and their widespread acceptance by employers are making it increasingly difficult to land a job as a paralegal—particularly in a large law firm—without any formal training.

That's not to say that it's impossible to obtain a job without it. It's been the practice of small law firms to promote legal secretaries to paralegals or to hire people without a paralegal certificate and train them on the job. But be forewarned: This is changing. For the most part, the days when you can walk in and be hired as a paralegal without any formal training are over.

On-the-Job Training

Whatever program you choose, formal training and education are only one component of becoming a paralegal. They provide the foundation of knowledge but not the day-to-day skills you need for success. As in any profession, these important skills must be learned on the job.

Anyone who's in the workforce will tell you that there's no substitute for on-the-job training. It's difficult to simulate the real situations working paralegals face in a classroom. Unfortunately, on-the-job training means anything from formal, in-house training programs to the take-the-ball-and-run approach. I have experienced both and will take formal, in-house training any day.

In-house training. Many law firms provide newly hired paralegals with in-house training and orientation programs. These programs introduce newcomers to the profession to basic legal concepts; specific tasks, such as summarizing depositions; computer systems; and management techniques. Programs are administered by a paralegal manager, an attorney, or a combination of both. The most successful programs have the support of the firm's partners, associates, and management.

Training often employs the use of "systems" binders for instruction in the procedures of a specific legal task, such as preparing a will. A binder will contain:

- Written step-by-step procedures

- Standardized forms

- Checklists

- Source materials

- Sample form letters

- Information regarding preparation of documents

- Master information containing basic data on a particular case

In addition to the systems binder, training may also include assignments based on hypothetical problems that are critiqued by the paralegal manager upon completion. Typically, new paralegals are also trained in legal research and writing and the use of LEXIS or WESTLAW and the law library.

Career Tip

Obviously, the larger the firm, the more resources it will have to devote to training programs. Paralegals hired by small firms and by corporations with small legal departments usually don't have the luxury of in-house programs. Those are the firms that generally hand off the ball and want you to run with it.

Susan Roe, paralegal coordinator at a San Francisco law firm, uses another approach to training that's been quite successful. "The entry-level paralegals are put through a training program that lasts one week. We teach them what to look for during discovery, how to summarize depositions, do a document production, use the law library, cite check, *Shepardize*, and Bates stamp. However, initially they aren't allowed to do these things on their own. Training is followed by a buddy or mentor system where they're assigned to a senior paralegal. The buddy system works well because the junior paralegal is learning while the senior paralegal is teaching."

CONTINUING EDUCATION

While continuing education applies to working paralegals who want to stay abreast of the trends and developments in the field, it's important to understand that continuing education should be an integral part of all paralegal careers. It is the supplement to both formal and informal education and training that helps paralegals keep up with the ever-changing laws and regulations in their particular specialty.

Legal Assistant Today's 1996 salary survey reported that 61 percent of the paralegals who responded received reimbursement for continuing legal education. These programs are offered through paralegal and bar associations as well as proprietary paralegal schools.

CLA Designation

Continuing education may also be used to maintain designation as a certified legal assistant (CLA). The CLA designation, first established in 1976, is bestowed by the National Association of Legal Assistants (NALA) as professional recognition of paralegals who have achieved and maintain a particular level of competence in the field. It is not the same as a paralegal certificate, which is awarded by an educational institution. The CLA designation is a voluntary certification program awarded by NALA exclusively and is based on an applicant's performance on NALA-administered tests.

To sit for the NALA tests, prospective CLA candidates must first meet specific requirements relating to education and/or experience. For further information on these requirements, contact NALA headquarters at 918-587-6828.

The designation is granted after successful completion of a comprehensive two-day exam that covers communications, ethics, human relations and interviewing techniques, judgment and analytical ability, legal research, legal terminology, and substantive law. The substantive law section consists of five examinations covering the American legal system and four of the following areas of practice: administrative law, criminal law and procedure, bankruptcy law, litigation, probate and estate planning, contracts, real estate, and business organizations/corporate. The CLA credential must be renewed every five years.

An advanced certificate in the areas of bankruptcy, civil litigation, corporations/business law, criminal law and procedure, intellectual property, estate planning and probate, and real estate is available to those who have achieved the CLA credential. NALA is working with various states to establish an advanced specialty certification program to test knowledge of state law and procedure. Programs are already available in Florida, Louisiana, and California.

PACE (Paralegal Advanced Competency Exam)

During the NFPA's 1994 Mid-Year Meeting, the membership voted to develop an exam to test the competency of experienced practicing paralegals. This was done both to advance the profession by acknowledging the role paralegals are providing in the legal services industry as well as to respond to those states considering regulation of the paralegal profession.

The Paralegal Advanced Competency Exam (PACE) was first given in July 1996. Since the NFPA now recommends a four-year degree for entering the profession, it has set a bachelor's degree as the cornerstone for exam qualification. To sit for Tier 1 of the PACE exam (Tier 1 includes general legal issues and ethics), paralegals need a four-year degree and completion of a paralegal program within an institutionally accredited school, plus at least two years of paralegal work experience. (It should be noted that the American Association for Paralegal Education [AAfPE] objects to the four-year degree requirement to sit for the PACE exam.)

The PACE can be taken six days a week at over 200 Sylvan Learning Centers nationwide. To apply for the exam, contact NFPA at P.O. Box 33108, Kansas City, Missouri 64114-0108 or 816-941-4000 to obtain a copy of the Candidates Handbook for $15. This charge is deducted from the exam fee of $225. In addition, daylong PACE review seminars are available and are sponsored by the NFPA and its member associations and are offered throughout the United States. For further information contact NFPA at the above address and telephone number.

Advanced Specialty Testing

Both the NALA and the NFPA are providing for advanced specialty testing. Paralegals who have earned the CLA designation are eligible for NALA's specialty certification, which began in 1982. To be certified as a specialist, a paralegal must pass an exam in his or her specialty area. Specialty certification is given in the areas of civil litigation, probate and estate planning, corporate and business law, criminal law and procedure, real estate, and bankruptcy.

In December 1995, the California Advanced Specialty (CAS) exam was first offered by NALA in cooperation with the California Alliance of

Paralegal Associations (CAPA). The exam was developed specifically for California certified legal assistants (CLAs) and is specific to California law and procedure. The CAS credential must be renewed every five years.

The NFPA also offers advanced testing in specialty areas in Tier II of the PACE exam. Requirements to sit for Tier II include successful completion of Tier I plus two additional years of paralegal experience.

Career Tip

It's worth noting that employers often advertise for certified paralegals when they really want paralegals with certificates—not CLA designations.

Because standardized paralegal education and training programs have not been adopted industrywide, entry into the field is available through a variety of programs to individuals with a wide range of experiences. But it's clear that a combination of formal paralegal education, on-the-job training, and good communication skills—as well as a dose of common sense—will provide you with all the tools you need to succeed in this challenging and rewarding field. And, although this chapter has only touched on the importance of computer literacy, it is an area of expertise that will become more vital to the profession in the years to come. For that reason, the next chapter is devoted entirely to that part of paralegal education.

CHAPTER 6

Taking the Byte Out of Computers:
Computer Basics and Beyond for Paralegals

The art of progress is to preserve order amid change and to preserve change amid order.
Alfred North Whitehead

■

Imagine that you're a paralegal with several years of experience behind you. You've just begun a new job working for a major corporation. One of your primary responsibilities is to administer the company's executive stock option program, which has recently been converted from a manual system to a computer. Although your specialty is in the area of stock options, you don't know anything about computers. (Also, the attorneys know less than you do about them and have no desire to learn—that's why they hired you.) To make matters worse, you learn you won't be receiving any computer training from the company and are expected to figure out what you have to do on your own.

You sit down at the computer and turn it on. Unfortunately, the software vendor whose program you are using provides minimal customer support, and the user manual is sketchy, outdated, couched in computerese, and not much help. The test of wits between you and the machine begins. You try every combination of keystrokes but are met with obnoxious bells, buzzers, and flashing lights—all signifying ERROR!

This is the wonderful world of computers you've heard so much about?

Meanwhile, the controller of the company is waiting for a printout of officers' stock options, which the computer supposedly generates in less than 5 minutes. Three hours later the controller has his report, you have ten more gray hairs, and the thought of heading to the nearest exit enters your mind. You persevere, however. After several more hair-raising episodes over the next few months, not only do you learn how to use the computer and all its software, but it becomes your friend and ally. Ultimately, you become a full-fledged computer junkie. You're hooked!

This scenario describes my introduction to computers in 1984, using the "trial-and-error" method of training. I wouldn't recommend this "method" to anyone. Back in 1984 the application of computers to law was still in its infancy. While this is no longer the case, the point is that you should not be caught without computer skills. In fact, the use of computers in the practice of law has created one of the fastest-growing areas of paralegal specialization.

THE LEGAL PROFESSION DISCOVERS COMPUTERS

According to a 1996 study by the American Bar Association's Legal Technology Resource Center on the impact of computers in law firms, 84 percent of attorneys who responded use a computer, compared to 59 percent in 1990. In order to understand why these numbers are so impressive, a little background on the development of computers in law might be helpful. For the most part, lawyers are interested in practicing law, not managing their law practices. To some lawyers, computers are just a necessary evil. It has only been quite recently that lawyers have come to realize the benefits of using them. Compared to other industries, the legal profession has been slow to implement the use of computers in its day-to-day operations.

Computers first began to appear in law firms between 1970 and 1980 with the purchase of word processing and billing systems. The current standard for word processing centers found in medium and large law firms today began during this time. For example, in some firms, documents over ten pages are sent to a word processing center, while those under ten pages are handled by a secretary. This arrangement provides both attorneys and paralegals with a quick turnaround time and frees up secretaries for other tasks. This allows law firms to charge clients an hourly rate for word processing as well, and it can be extremely profitable.

Just as significant as the introduction of word processing was the introduction of computerized billing systems. As discussed in earlier chapters, accurate recording of billable hours for attorneys, paralegals, and support staff is crucial to a firm's profitability. As caseloads increased and clients demanded more detailed invoices, the need for efficient billing systems became apparent. Since these systems ran on expensive mainframes and minicomputers, they were initially purchased by the larger law firms.

As the decade moved toward the 1980s, firms began to purchase more sophisticated equipment: optical character readers, computerized telephone systems, facsimile machines, laser printers, computerized legal research systems such as LEXIS and WESTLAW, and photocopiers that track client charges.

Computerized litigation support systems also emerged in this period, making it possible to do a rapid electronic search through thousands of documents to locate information that can be used in preparation for a trial. In the past, a manual search for the same information would take days or even weeks! Originally only the very large law firms used such systems because they only ran on expensive mainframes that were not particularly user friendly. IBM changed all that with its introduction of the personal computer (PC). The relatively low cost of this technology made it possible to computerize the office systems of small firms and sole practitioners who couldn't afford the expensive mainframes.

The first systems transferred to PCs were word processing, billing, accounting, legal research, and calendaring. During this time, law firms began using local area networks (LANs) for the purpose of sharing word processing files and printers between secretaries. As PCs became more powerful in the middle to late 1980s, litigation support and document management systems were transferred from mainframes to PCs. This has proved to be one of the most significant developments for the legal industry in general and for litigation paralegals in particular.

The 1990s have seen the introduction of a number of hardware and software technologies to the legal profession, including CD-ROMs, imaging systems, groupware, videoconferencing, courtroom animation software, wide area networks (WANs), e-mail, online services, voice recognition, intranets, and the Internet.

Other recent innovations include the use of document assembly or expert system software to draft documents in substantive practice areas of law, such as estate planning, tax, corporate, and real estate, to name a few.

> ## *Some Helpful Hints for New Computer Users*
>
> The following advice may be helpful to remember when you're dealing with computers.
>
> - It's difficult to keep up with the myriad products introduced by the computer industry each week—don't even try.
> - Every piece of hardware and software is different, and most require trial-and-error training. (Surprisingly, this is the method used by the most experienced computer professionals.)
> - Computer training is not a given anymore. Most paralegal employers will expect you to have a great deal of computer literacy.
> - Don't be surprised if you don't understand everything about computers after you receive training. You never will.
> - Attorneys generally know less about computers than you do and will rely on you to become the expert.
> - The user manual doesn't explain everything. Inevitably, the thing you most need to know won't be in it. You might find it worthwhile to buy a guidebook for your specific software program to supplement the information in your user manual. Numerous books have been published on each of the popular software programs, and most people find them more complete and much easier to follow than the manuals that come with the software.
> - When you think nothing else could possibly go wrong, be assured that it always will!

Technology Issues and Trends Facing the Legal Profession

As a new paralegal, your career will be directly affected by some of the technology issues and trends facing the legal profession today. The proliferation of technology in the law is perhaps best seen at one of the dozens of legal technology shows presented throughout the United States each year.

I recently attended Legal Tech—New York, presented by Price Waterhouse, where the theme was "Legal Tech—The Second Decade: Winning with Technology." To give you some idea of the technology issues and trends facing the legal industry today, the following are some sample focus sessions and seminars presented at the show:

Intranets for Litigation Management
Task-Based Billing: What to do with all the data

Courtroom Technology: Integrating technology into trial practice
Discovery of Electronically Stored Information
Groupware in the Practice of Law
Internet Security and Risks
On The Desktop: Windows 95 or Windows NT

It is important to note that a good deal of the technology developed for the legal industry, particularly the software, centers around the practice area of litigation. This was evident just leafing through the show's program guide, as well as visiting dozens of vendor booths.

The *AmLaw Tech* Survey published in the Fall 1996 issue of *AmLaw Tech* magazine studied hardware and software usage in the 100 largest U.S. firms, ranked by gross revenue. Key question areas included dominant platform; percent using laptops; wide area network (WAN) usage; whether they are using Windows, Windows 95, or Windows NT; intranet usage; and what types of software they are using for document management, word processing, litigation support, and imaging.

The survey found that most firms are using IBM-compatible PCs, either 486s or Pentiums, with wide area networks to link all of their offices. The percentage of lawyers using laptops in lieu of desktop PCs ranges anywhere from 0 to 99 percent, depending on the firm. Most firms use Microsoft Windows, with plans to move to Windows 95 or Windows NT in the near future. The most common software products used were PC Docs or SoftSolutions for document management and either Word-Perfect or Word for word processing. A variety of products were used for litigation support and imaging. However, cutting-edge technologies such as intranets and groupware like Lotus Notes were not used extensively. Additional findings and trends included:

- Dramatic shift from DOS to Windows, with 76 percent of firms using Windows (up from 32 percent in 1994 survey)

- WordPerfect, once the dominant word processor, is losing ground to Microsoft Word

- Demand for portability is increasing, with laptops becoming the PC of choice

- Use of e-mail has exploded, allowing attorneys to communicate between themselves and their clients

- Emphasis is shifting from desktop computing to firmwide networks, with 71 percent firms wanting to enhance infrastructure and connectivity

Perhaps the most surprising finding of all was the shift in attitude toward computers from the 1994 to the 1996 survey. In just two years, the survey found that a profession once wary about computers has now become an outspoken advocate for them. This attitude can best be summed up by John Tredennick Jr., litigation partner and chief information officer of Denver's Holland & Hart, who said that "Technology is a competitive weapon, not just some backroom phenomena."

The Internet and Intranets

Despite the legal industry's slow acceptance of technology in the past, as a whole it has been relatively quick to embrace the Internet. Evidence of this can be seen in the results of one of the most comprehensive surveys on Internet use in the legal industry ever done. In the fall of 1996, *The Internet Lawyer* magazine surveyed Internet use among a random sample of lawyers, paralegals, legal administrators, law librarians, and law firm MIS directors. The Internet Lawyer-Microsoft Corporation Survey found that 71 percent of all respondents use the Internet. The most common applications were e-mail, research, and online marketing opportunities. Eighty-five percent of respondents said their use of the Internet would increase in the future.

On the other hand, the 1996 *AmLaw Tech* survey found that despite the fact that most firms have access to the Internet, for the most part many are using it only for e-mail. Some firms are concerned with issues involving security, accuracy of information, and the inability to monitor what is being accessed. It remains to be seen whether the Internet will become the preferred method for obtaining information. But one thing is clear: the Internet has made its mark on the legal industry and is here to stay.

Not catching on quite as rapidly as the Internet phenomena are intranets, which are in-house Web pages that give employees easier access to the firm's information, forms, and files. The 1996 *AmLaw Tech* survey found that only 21 percent of law firms are designing their own intranets. One firm is using it to navigate the World Wide Web itself. For example, it uses a standard Web browser to call up its internal Web page, which contains links to sites useful for legal research. Over the next few years, intranet usage is predicted to increase, particularly in large firms where disseminating information firmwide is important.

COMPUTERS AND THE PARALEGAL

Lawyers are in the business of providing information, both verbal and written. It is the paralegal's responsibility to organize and manage the written form as effectively and efficiently as possible. Before computers, this was a cumbersome task and one that led to burnout. Computers have definitely lengthened the career of many a paralegal.

Paralegals are among a law firm's most intensive computer users. Some on-the-job computer applications commonly encountered by paralegals today include:

- Word processing
- Research (legal and factual)
- Litigation support, case management, and databases
- Courtroom technology
- Calendaring
- Document assembly

Of course, the specific applications used depend on where the paralegal works (such as in a law firm, corporation, or government agency, to name a few), legal specialty area, the degree of automation within the organization, and, more important, the organization's attitude toward automation. For instance, case management, litigation support, and courtroom graphics programs would be used primarily by litigation paralegals.

In a 1996 survey on computers and paralegals, *Legal Assistant Today* magazine reports the percentage of paralegals using computers for the following applications:

Drafting documents 94%
Legal research 60%
Calendaring 52%
Litigation support 50%
Database 49%
Summarize depositions 43%
Case management 40%
Document assembly 35%

Additional applications included: cite checking 31%, mail merging 29%, full-text retrieval 24%, redlining 23%, collections 13%, conflicts checking 13%, and imaging 10%.

Word Processing

Before the introduction of PCs in the mid-1980s, most paralegals used a secretary for all their word processing needs. The only exception were those paralegals working in the smaller law firms who also functioned as secretaries. Now most paralegals have PCs on their desks and are doing their own word processing. Depending on the firm, these PCs are either standalone or networked.

You should be aware of the debate currently raging in the legal industry over which word processing application firms are using: WordPerfect or Microsoft Word. Until recently, WordPerfect was the dominant word processor in the legal industry, due in part to the industry's use of DOS as the PC operating system. When law firms began to shift to Windows in the last few years, they started using Microsoft Word. There is some resistance to this shift by staff who have used WordPerfect for years, and it has caused law firms a great deal of time and expense for re-training. It's wise to be aware that while many firms are still using WordPerfect, most are planning to move to Word in the near future.

Research

Paralegals spend a good part of their time searching for, accessing, and retrieving information. For the past two decades, the use of online databases greatly increased the scope and accuracy of finding this information. Recently, law libraries on CD-ROM have become very popular because they make research so much easier and quicker. It is estimated that approximately 1 hour of computerized research is roughly equal to 9 or 10 hours of traditional research in the law library. And the latest innovation in legal research is the use of the Internet, which contains dozens of sites relating to federal, state, and local statutory and case law.

There are two types of computer-assisted research conducted by paralegals: legal and general information.

Legal research. As I explained in Chapter 3, legal research is a search for authorities in the law—more specifically, for statutes or court decisions, or both, from a particular jurisdiction—that are applicable to a particular legal situation. The substance of a legal search, whether it is conducted traditionally or is computer aided, is always the same. What varies is the method by which it is undertaken.

After a problem is analyzed in terms of predetermined categories such as torts, negligence, or conspiracy, the traditional method requires going to a law library to locate the books, indexes, and digests that refer to the desired cases. A computer-assisted search begins with an analysis as well, but the follow-up requires using a database.

The major advantage of computer-assisted legal research (CALR) is timeliness. If covered by a database, a court decision (or any other information) will be available online almost as soon as it is known. While the information would eventually be available in a law library, the time required for printing, publishing, and distribution delays its accessibility.

Today, legal research is conducted using a variety of methods including CD-ROM libraries, online services, and more recently, the Internet. The two oldest online subscription services for performing legal research are LEXIS and WESTLAW, but there are other similar services and CD-ROM libraries now. Such services and CD-ROMs provide federal and state databases that are made up of cases and statutes. The researcher inputs a search request of words, phrases, or numbers, and the online service or CD-ROM searches the applicable databases to retrieve the case or statute "on point" (the case or statute that most closely resembles the one that's being worked on in terms of legal principles). Cases can be retrieved in various formats: full text, partial text, or citation. Such services and CD-ROM libraries can also be used for cite checking and *Shepardizing*, as discussed in Chapter 3.

How much and how often a paralegal uses CD-ROMs or online services such as LEXIS depends on two factors: work environment and area of legal specialty. Paralegals who work at law firms generally do more legal research than those employed by corporations or government agencies. This is because paralegals in law firms work for several clients simultaneously and are more apt to use an online service on a daily basis. Those employed by corporations or government agencies usually work with outside counsel and that counsel does the majority of the research.

The paralegal's specialty area also plays a significant role in determining how he or she uses online services and CD-ROM libraries. Many paralegals first encounter LEXIS while working in litigation since it depends heavily on case law and precedent. In this area, LEXIS is used to search for statutes and case law, to cite check, and to *Shepardize*.

LEXIS can also be used by paralegals who specialize in securities, probate, tax law, patents, or trademarks. For instance, the LEXPAT database, which contains information on hundreds of patents and trademarks, can be used to do a patent search.

General information research. In addition to legal research, the paralegal also conducts factual research. Before the introduction of the Internet, paralegals used online services to access a variety of databases to conduct factual research. These services are available via subscription and provide access to a wide variety of sources for business, education, technology, science, health, and travel information. Many also provide the full text of articles from newspapers and magazines.

The information in these databases can be extremely useful to the practice of law. For instance, if an attorney wants to know if the firm's client, let's say General Motors, has been mentioned in the news during the last six months in reference to a potential takeover by Ford, a paralegal can scan the *New York Times* and *Wall Street Journal* databases for articles referring to General Motors and Ford.

An alternative to using expensive online services to perform legal research is to purchase a CD-ROM library. The advantage to using CD-ROMs to do research is the decrease in cost from the online services. The disadvantage is that new cases and information are not updated as rapidly as they are with an online service. In addition, research done using a CD-ROM library is only as good as the search engine available.

Research using the Internet. A relatively recent phenomena is the use of the Internet to perform legal or factual research. The fall 1996 survey by the newsletter *The Internet Lawyer* found that 55 percent of all paralegals responding to the survey use the Internet. One of the more interesting findings was that 76 percent of all those responding use the Internet for legal research. Some of the more commonly used legal sites included the Cornell Legal Information Institute (www.law.cornell.edu), the Library of Congress (www.loc.gov), and the American Bar Association (www.aba.org). When asked whether they would be willing to switch from traditional legal online services such as WESTLAW and LEXIS to Internet access, 35 percent of respondents said they would be very likely to switch.

As new legal-related sites become available, the Internet will become an increasingly viable option for performing research. One expert suggested that for the small-firm lawyer, the following two Internet sites would replace any need for CD-ROM libraries: Versus (www.versuslaw.com) and Lois (www.pita.com). Both sites offer low-cost federal and state information.

Whether the Internet will replace online services, such as LEXIS, as the preferred method of research remains to be seen. While information on the Internet is free (online subscription services charge a sizable fee), issues such as accuracy of information, security, access speed, and searching capabilities are still of concern to some law firms.

The preferred method—computer-assisted research—is being used by attorneys and paralegals more than ever today, due in large part to the accessibility of the Internet, expanded databases, reduced online costs, and increased acceptance of the technology by the legal profession in general. While a greater percentage of research is now being conducted using CD-ROMs, online databases such as LEXIS, or the Internet, the traditional method of research using books has not yet become obsolete. However, legal publishers are rushing to convert their printed material to CD-ROMs and are beginning to make it available on the Internet. In the not so distant future, we may see a paperless law library. In fact, one expert advised new attorneys starting out not to purchase law books at all.

Litigation Support, Case Management, and Databases

Case management software, better known as automated litigation support systems (ALSS), is a computerized method of rapidly managing, accessing, and retrieving information and documents over the course of a case using database technology. A database consists of four components: inputs (data collection and entry), processing (information sorting), output (reports), and control (mechanisms to ensure system security and performance).

One of the primary functions of an ALSS is to support the discovery phase of a lawsuit, which, in some cases, can last for years. (Discovery is the tool that allows both parties to discover everything there is to know about the opposition's case.) This is accomplished by using various legal methods, including interrogatories, depositions, document productions, and requests for admissions. The power of an ALSS is its ability to convert the information in these documents to a database for quick access and retrieval.

Litigation paralegals use this software to organize, manage, access, and retrieve documents during the discovery phase of a lawsuit and also during the trial phase. With the search and sort functions of the database, a paralegal can prepare the witness book and the deposition exhibits that relate to particular witnesses and compile periodic updates to show the status of admitting documents into evidence and the like.

While case management software is often used by litigation paralegals to manage documents in a lawsuit, it can also be used by paralegals

111

working in transactional specialty areas. So it has not only changed the practice of litigation, but it has also made paralegal work in all specialty areas infinitely easier.

Over the last decade, dozens of companies have developed litigation support software for the PC. There are three types currently available: abstracting, full-text, and an integrated system that uses both.

Abstracting. Abstract database software is the most common type of litigation software used for letters, memos, and any document from which information can be summarized and abstracted. This is done by coding the information by subject matter and entering it into a database.

You can either purchase off-the-shelf systems or create your own. If a case is too small to warrant the expense of an off-the-shelf package, some computer-literate paralegals who have more advanced database programming skills can create their own proprietary databases.

In either case, a database must first be built with fields corresponding to key words, subjects, people, dates, and so on, depending on the relevant issues and facts in a case. A coding form might be developed corresponding to the database fields. Every document that is received is then analyzed, coded, and entered into the various fields of the database. This is done either by the paralegal, or by coders often hired on a temporary basis just for this purpose.

Coding may be objective and/or subjective. Objective coding is limited to the information that appears on the document, such as date, author, and recipient. Subjective coding involves a substantive analysis of its content. The coder reads each document, extracts the relevant information, lists it on the coding form, and inputs the information into the appropriate database fields. At this stage, a paralegal may be responsible for reviewing the work of the coders to maintain quality control.

Once a sufficient database is built, an attorney or paralegal can use the ALSS to retrieve information and hard copy. A paralegal then creates and maintains the document retrieval system—an ALSS is of little use if hard copies of the documents referenced in the database can't be located. At this point, the paralegal is using the database software, which requires a more sophisticated level of computer skill.

The advantages to abstract systems include their ability to sort through large volumes of documents to access information as well as to produce reports. If coding and data entry standards are properly maintained, these systems provide accuracy and uniformity in retrieving information.

The downside to abstract programs is their inability to produce the actual document. Once a search is complete and a report produced, the document still needs to be retrieved. An additional detriment is the up-front time and cost involved in coding and data entry. This cost must be weighed against the time savings involved in not having to review voluminous amounts of information to obtain what an abstract system can provide.

Full-Text. The second type of litigation support software programs available is the full-text package. Full-text packages are used when it's necessary to have access to the entire text of a document—a deposition transcript, for example. In a case with one hundred volumes of depositions, the attorney might want to know all of the references to a particular client. A full-text search can be done and a list produced with all of the references.

Full-text software can also be used to summarize depositions. As mentioned in Chapter 3, summarizing depositions can be tedious and time consuming. With full-text software, a transcript is transferred to a diskette by a court reporter and then loaded into a computer. The summary is done quickly and easily by electronically scanning the full text for key words and phrases.

Until recently, the problem with full-text packages was that there were only two types of documents that could be viewed: documents of oral testimony such as depositions that were transcribed by a court reporter and then converted to ASCII (American Standard Code for Information Interchange) on diskette, or documents that could be read by an optical character reader (OCR).

The OCRs were somewhat limited because they could only scan certain typefaces and could not scan handwriting. A recent innovation in scanning devices called document imaging systems has solved the problem. Imaging devices are similar to photocopiers or fax machines—exact representations of documents can be made. Documents are then stored as images on either magnetic tape or laser disk, thus eliminating the need for hard copy—a paralegal's dream come true. The benefit is that all documents in a case can now be viewed, including those with handwriting on them.

The ability to search for exact language and testimony is the primary advantage of a full-text system over abstract programs. One of the downsides is the inconsistency in vocabulary used in these searches. Also, misspelled use of names can hamper a search.

Integration. The final type of software available is the integrated package, which offers both powerful databases for document abstracting and full-text capabilities. These packages represent the best of both worlds, allowing the user to manage a variety of different types of information including text, images, and multimedia.

Career Tip

A paralegal's responsibilities in the development, implementation, and maintenance of an automated litigation support system (ALSS) vary, depending on the resources of the law firm and its size, the complexity of the case, the attorneys' attitudes toward paralegals, and the number of support staff assigned to the ALSS project. Duties can range from simple information classification and coding to subjective, substantive analysis of documents.

Courtroom Technology

The courtroom of the 1990s and beyond is becoming high tech. The public was introduced to some of the most innovative courtroom technology during the O. J. Simpson trial: computerized transcripts, graphics and animation, and 3-D scale models. These intriguing applications of technology to the legal profession is also an expanding area of opportunity for paralegals.

A recent innovation is the introduction of real-time court reporting. This is where a court reporter's stenographic notes are instantaneously converted into the English language and projected onto computer monitors for all to read. In the past, these notes had to be translated overnight for distribution the next day in hard-copy form. The time saved with this new technology is enormous.

The judicial electronic document and data interchange (JEDDI) system is rapidly being implemented in law offices and courtrooms across the country. JEDDI allows lawyers and paralegals to file and retrieve pleadings electronically without leaving their offices. Until recently, the idea of a paperless courtroom was only a dream. Now it is a reality, particularly in Delaware, which requires that all documents in asbestos and complex insurance cases be filed electronically.

The preparation of trial exhibits using graphics software is a growing area of expertise for computer-literate litigation paralegals. Recall from Chapter 3 that one of a litigation paralegal's responsibilities is to create the trial exhibits in a case. Trial exhibits come in many forms, including written excerpts from documents, photographs, charts, and graphs. In recent years, more sophisticated animation and graphics software programs have enhanced their explanations, making it easier for juries to understand them. These software packages make it possible for the paralegal to create trial exhibits in-house. Paralegals with expertise in such software are invaluable to a firm.

In the past five years, more and more attorneys are using computer animation to enhance their cases. This is a technique in which a series of computer-generated images (graphics) are successively recorded on videotape. When the tape is played, it provides the added dimension of motion and time to what would otherwise be a stationary object. The applications of computer animation are particularly useful to personal injury and product liability cases where an accident must be recreated or a product must be illustrated in three dimensions.

Laser disk technology, first developed in the late 1970s, is another innovation being used in the practice of law. Laser disks store large amounts of multimedia images, including visual, auditory, and printed material, that can be retrieved instantaneously. They hold images of all types, including photographs, charts, documents, live video segments, computer animations, audio segments, or any combination thereof. They are increasingly being used in the courtroom to enhance the presentation of evidence and to tell a client's story. These products synchronize videotaped images of a deposition with the corresponding testimony. During a trial, when a lawyer searches for a word or phrase from the testimony, the corresponding video image simultaneously appears on the screen. This new technology now makes it possible for a juror to see how the witness reacted to questions asked at a deposition.

Prior to this technology, when an attorney examined a witness and referred to a particular document, the paralegal had to search through cartons of documents to retrieve the hard copy. Now with the press of a button, a letter, exhibit, or videotaped deposition instantly appears on a television monitor.

While all of these technologies are very useful and clever innovations, some are costly, and not all law firms can justify using them for all cases. However, as the cost decreases, more and more law firms will need to use these software programs to stay competitive. Given the continued litigious nature of our society, paralegals with expertise in these areas will continue to be in demand.

Calendaring

Not quite as exciting as courtroom technology but just as important are software packages that automate the calendaring function. Imagine a law firm with over three hundred cases in varying stages of discovery and trial. The rules of civil procedure that govern the procedures for trying a case have very specific time limitations regarding pleadings, motions, and court proceedings. The consequences of not filing a pleading on time can be devastating, as I, myself, have witnessed on several occasions.

Other events that are calendared include administrative proceedings, depositions, and client meetings, to name just a few. Without a tickler system, it would be almost impossible to keep track of these events with any accuracy.

Depending on the size of the law firm, you may or may not be responsible for the calendaring function. Most large firms have an individual solely responsible for generating and distributing a calendar on a daily basis. Even so, some paralegals create their own calendaring system, either by using a standard database or by purchasing an off-the-shelf program.

In addition, there are products now available that integrate calendaring with litigation support, word processing, and conflict-of-interest checking, all with access to LEXIS and WESTLAW legal research databases. They are one-stop-shopping software systems.

Document assembly

As mentioned earlier, the *Legal Assistant Today* 1996 computer survey found that 94 percent of paralegals responding used computers to draft documents. This was the number one use of computers by paralegals. A recent innovation is the trend toward automating the preparation of documents in specific practice areas. One such technology, called document assembly, assists the user in assembling documents in a variety of practice areas, such as business, employment, family law, estate planning, to name just a few. Specific documents assembled might be employment agreements, wills, incorporation documents, or marital settlement agreements.

Document assembly programs can range from a simple forms-on-disk package, where the user does no more than fill in the blanks, to programs using a question and answer process where the answers are translated into documents. The latest innovation in document assembly software is called expert systems, where intelligence is added to the question and answer process. As the user answers each question, he or she can access legal analysis, strategy, and practice tips prepared by an expert in that particular area of law. These software programs combine legal research, decision support, and document drafting in one process and are the cutting edge in document assembly technology today.

Word processing, legal and factual research, case management, litigation support, courtroom technology, calendaring, and document assembly are just some of the ways paralegals are interacting with computers. Not only are paralegals becoming adept at using these systems, but they are also creating their own proprietary programs. In addition, many paralegals are performing managerial and supervisory functions relating to computer applications such as:

- Performing a requirements analysis to determine appropriate hardware and software needs;
- Selecting vendors and products;
- Acting as liaison between attorneys and vendors;
- Training coworkers in software procedures; and
- Supervising temporary coders in the development of litigation support systems.

As PCs become more powerful and software becomes more sophisticated, paralegals will inevitably create new uses for computers in the practice of law.

COMPUTER SKILLS FOR PARALEGALS

The computer applications discussed in this chapter all require varying levels of expertise. But just how computer literate do you need to be? That will depend on your specialty area as well as where you work.

Given the pace at which the computer industry introduces new products each year, you will encounter many different information system (IS) configurations. The type and amount of equipment a law firm has is directly dependent on its size, its budget, and, most importantly, the attitude of the attorneys toward computers. Most firms these days, whether large or small, use some kind of local area network (LAN). The larger firms are also linked via wide area networks (WANs). Very few firms these days are working exclusively on stand-alone PCs.

For the most part, paralegals have little to do with mainframes and minicomputers; almost, if not all, of their computer work is done on PCs. You'll find most firms using IBMs and IBM-compatibles rather than the

Apple Macintosh PCs, although some firms use Macs to produce high-quality graphics for trial preparation.

Until recently, the majority of the legal industry was still using DOS as the standard operating system for IBM and IBM-compatible PCs. Now most law firms are using Microsoft's Windows and many will be upgrading to Windows 95 in the near future.

Career Tip

Attention Mac users: Since most law offices use personal computers, if you are a devoted Mac user, I would highly advise becoming proficient on the personal computer using Microsoft's Windows 95 operating system.

There are two categories of PC software that law firms use today. The first type involves the generic, off-the-shelf packages for word processing, spreadsheets, databases, graphics, and desktop publishing packages with which many of us are familiar.

The second category is the application-specific software discussed in this chapter for tasks such as case management, litigation support, and calendaring as well as the more innovative software that automates procedures in specific practice areas, such as document assembly programs.

No matter where you work or what specialty area you work in, at a minimum, you will be expected to know how to use the following types of programs and applications: word processing, spreadsheet, database, presentation and graphics, CD-ROMs, e-mail, online research programs, and the Internet.

The specific programs you use will depend on what the firm is using at the time. While Microsoft, Corel, and Lotus all offer office suites of products, the trend is toward Microsoft's Office 95 or Office 97, which include Word (word processing), Excel (spreadsheet), PowerPoint (presentation graphics), and Access (database).

The following are some of the more common software packages used by paralegals today:

- Word processing: Word, WordPerfect
- Spreadsheets: Excel, Quattro Pro, Lotus 1-2-3
- Databases: Access, Paradox, dbase
- Graphics/Desktop publishing: Adobe PageMaker, Harvard Graphics, Adobe Illustrator, Microsoft PowerPoint

- Document management: PC Docs, SoftSolutions
- Litigation support: Summation, Concordance, Folio View, Discovery Magic
- Time and billing: TimeSlips
- Contact management: ACT, MS Schedule+, Time Matters, Goldmine
- Legal research: LEXIS, WESTLAW, West CD-ROM Libraries
- Accounting: Quickbooks, Quickbooks Pro (paralegals in smaller firms sometimes also handle bookkeeping)

Computer training is available from many different sources, including college courses, all-day seminars, on-site training, software tutorials, and, as a last resort, the software manual. I prefer an intensive all-day seminar, supplemented with exercises to practice on your own over a period of several weeks. College courses are less expensive, but they tend to drag on over an entire semester. On-site training is great, but companies and law firms generally are reluctant to foot the bill. Software tutorials from user manuals are okay for beginners, but they are limiting—you can't ask a computer questions.

The point is, don't wait until after you've been hired in your first paralegal job to get computer training. You need to come to the position with as much knowledge as possible, particularly in the generic software programs. You will not be expected to know the legal-specific programs. These you will learn on the job.

PARALEGALS, TECHNOLOGY, AND THE FUTURE

There is little doubt that the legal profession is embracing technology more now than every before. The skepticism and resignation toward technology in the 1980s have been replaced by the belief that lawyers cannot compete without technology.

For those with computer expertise, there is no better time to be entering the paralegal profession than today. The transition to Windows as well as the decrease in cost and increase in speed of PCs have created dozens of innovative legal technology applications creating exciting opportunities for paralegals.

Paralegals are the perfect link between the attorney who knows little about computers and the computer specialist who knows nothing about the law. I believe that in the future, computer-literate paralegals will become more involved in providing in-house software support, developing new in-house computer applications, and training professional and support staff. They will also become more proactive in creating new technology-related positions within law firms.

For instance, with the increasing acceptance of the Internet, the possibility of a new position called the Internet paralegal could arise as a new subspecialty. Paralegals with specific expertise managing and accessing information and performing research on the Internet would be invaluable to law firms.

In the past few years, most law firms have come to recognize the importance of computers in the practice of law. The downsizing of the legal profession, as well as an increase in competition for clients, has made technology necessary for increasing both productivity and profitability. Paralegals will play a vital role in bridging the worlds of law and technology.

By now you have enough information about education, training, skills, and computer expertise to consider a job search. The next chapter explores a number of ways to begin.

CHAPTER 7

How Do You Find the Right Job?

There is no security on this earth. Only opportunity.
Douglas McArthur

■

You've now come to one of life's little pleasures: the job hunt. Gone are the days when you could learn a trade, work at one company for thirty-five years, receive a healthy pension, and retire worry-free. Many people will change careers—let alone jobs—several times before they retire. Since there are dozens of excellent how-to-land-a-job books on the market that offer valuable advice, I've tried not to be redundant. By offering information specifically related to the paralegal occupation, this chapter begins where those other books leave off.

JOB HUNTING TODAY

The recession of the early 1990s had a significant impact on the legal profession. For the first time, law firms began experiencing layoffs, mergers, consolidations, and even bankruptcies. In the past few years, though, an improved economy has meant more stabilization and less job layoffs in all professions. This is good news for entry-level paralegals, who are finding that opportunities for employment are increasing.

Legal Assistant Today magazine's second annual school placement survey reported that 65 percent of the 1995 graduates found jobs within three months of graduation, 77 percent after six months, and 83 percent after twelve months. An overwhelming 91 percent of the thirty-three program directors surveyed said that the paralegal job market was good to very strong. The few that were more pessimistic were located in the Northeast. Even in that region, one director said that paralegals were more in demand than associates.

The study concluded that one reason for the optimism was the increase in nontraditional jobs that are opening up for paralegals. For example, the placement office of one Colorado paralegal program noted that 30–40 percent of the requests it received for entry-level positions were outside of the traditional law firms and government agencies. One such request was by one law school for an audiovisual technical assistant—a perfect position for a paralegal with technical expertise.

The schools also reported that the majority of job offers for the more traditional positions came from small- and medium-size law firms with from one to fifty attorneys, not the large firms that were offering most of the traditional positions in the 1980s.

While these statistics are encouraging, you still need to be flexible in your job search. At a talk I gave to a paralegal internship class at a San Francisco Bay Area university, one student complained that he could not find a paralegal job. When I asked if he had looked in San Francisco, about 45 miles away, he said he hadn't because of the commute. I advised him to expand his job search to San Francisco, endure the commute for a year or so in order to get the job on his résumé, and then look for his next job closer to home. Being flexible like this can open up opportunities for you now that can lead to better jobs later on.

WHAT DO EMPLOYERS WANT?

In the 1980s when business was booming, employers were not as selective about the education, experience, and skills of new hires. But the recession of the early 1990s, an increase in graduates from paralegal training programs, and a growing pool of qualified, experienced paralegals have changed all that. The following are some hiring trends as they relate to education requirements, skill level, and legal specialty area.

Educational Requirements

The paralegal profession is struggling to define standards for education and training that can be accepted industrywide. While requirements for paralegal jobs vary from employer to employer and from region to region, one important trend is emerging: No matter what the firm size or its region or specialty area, employers are requiring that the entry-level paralegals they hire have formal training—either a paralegal certificate, a four-year bachelor's degree, or both. Gone are the days when you could walk into a law firm with neither of these and get a job.

Acceptance of this standard is seen everywhere today in the paralegal field. The PACE exam, given by the National Federation of Paralegal Associations (NFPA), discussed in Chapter 5, requires individuals sitting for the exam to have a four-year degree. The NFPA's 1995 *Paralegal Compensation and Benefits Report* finds that 54 percent of paralegals responding to the survey had bachelor degrees and 85 percent had paralegal certificates. Paralegal managers participating in roundtable discussions led by Cheri Estrin at the 1996 annual meetings of the Legal Assistant Management Association (LAMA) in San Francisco and Richmond, Virginia, agreed that a four-year degree was essential, particularly in the larger firms. Opinions were split on the necessity of a paralegal certificate.

All managers who participated in the discussion agreed that voluntary certification, either the CLA or the PACE designation, was not required for employment. These designations were viewed as personal achievement measures only.

The message is clear: entry-level paralegals must obtain formal training in order to stay competitive. The nature of that training depends in part on the size of the firm and the region of the country but you will never go wrong with a four-year degree and some form of paralegal education.

Skills in Demand

No matter what career you choose, a good rule of thumb is to acquire as many skills as you can. Employers are looking for diversity and for individuals with multiple skills. Employers today have the upper hand and can pick and choose from a large pool of qualified applicants. The more you have to offer, the better. Besides the basic writing, research, and organizational abilities discussed in Chapter 5, additional skills might include such things as bilingual abilities (with Japanese and Spanish topping the list) and computer expertise of any kind, as we have seen in Chapter 6.

During the 1996 LAMA roundtable discussion on the paralegal profession, paralegal managers were asked to name the three top skills and qualities essential for obtaining a paralegal position. Some of the responses included:

- Technology skills, interpersonal skills, and a proven track record
- Writing skills, academic achievement, "life" skills
- Problem solving, flexibility, "can-do" attitude

One manager said that common sense was the single most important skill for the entry-level paralegal to have. (I totally agree!) Other successful qualities paralegals need to succeed included perseverance, patience, a positive attitude, attention to detail, and dedication to the work.

HIRING TRENDS

In the second edition of this book, I reported that the outlook for full-time permanent jobs at the entry level was not encouraging because of the weak economy and the availability of experienced paralegals. Since then, the situation has completely turned around for entry-level positions, thanks to the upturn in the economy and the trend among employers in most all professions to hire less experienced workers for less money.

The number of permanent jobs for entry-level paralegals has increased, but law firms are still relying on temporary paralegals—in many firms, more than ever before. If you're willing to work on a temporary basis, this is still an excellent way to land your first paralegal job.

What's Hot and What's Not

At the 1996 LAMA roundtable on the paralegal profession, paralegal managers listed the following specialty areas as "hot" and "not":

- Hot: corporate, including mergers and acquisitions, securities, intellectual property, banking, litigation (particularly computerized litigation), labor, and real estate

- Not: probate (it's only handled in smaller firms these days; larger firms are dropping this practice area)

Due to the improved economy, the demand for corporate and real estate paralegals has increased dramatically. This is in contrast to *Legal Assistant Today*'s 1992 survey of recruiters that listed corporate and real estate as two specialties that were "not hot." Keep in mind that these two practice areas—corporate and real estate—are more affected by economic cycles than other areas such as litigation, which is always in demand.

List of Top Firms

The following results are from *Legal Assistant Today*'s first annual Best Firms to Work for Survey, conducted in 1997. More than 71 percent of respondents to the survey said respect and employer support were the main reasons why they thought their firm was the best. Surprisingly, salary and benefits came in second.

Firms with 1–5 attorneys:

Brigham & Gaustad, Ukiah, CA
Richard Lee Cobb & Hall, P.C., El Paso, TX

Runners up:

Berger & Berger, Evansville, IN
Law Office of Stephen H. DeBaun, Tucker, GA
Dempsey & Kingsland, P.C., Kansas City, MO
Dijulio & King, Glendale, CA
The Keenan Law Firm, Atlanta, GA
Komyatte & Freeland, P.C., Highland, IN
Mace J. Yampotsky, Ltd., Las Vegas, NV

Firms with 6–10 attorneys:

Boynton, Waldron, Doleac, Woodman & Scott, P.A., Portsmouth, NH
Moses, Wittemyer, Harrison & Woodruff, Boulder, CO

Firms with 11–50 attorneys:

Upton, Sanders & Smith, Concord, NH
Williams & Anderson, Little Rock, AR

Runners up:

Hanft, Pride, O'Brien, Harries, Swetbar & Burns, Duluth, MN
Hunter Richey DiBenedetto & Brewer, Sacramento, CA
Lewis & Kappes, Indianapolis, IN

Firms with 51–100 attorneys:

Miller, Johnson, Snell & Cummiskey, Grand Rapids, MI
Wright, Lindsey & Jennings, Little Rock, AR

Firms with 100+ attorneys:

Vorys, Sater, Seymour and Pease, Columbus, OH
Pennie & Edmonds, New York, NY

It is interesting to note that out of the twenty firms mentioned, twelve, or 60 percent, are located in the Midwest and South; five, or 25 percent, are from the West (California, Nevada, Colorado); and only three, or 15 percent, are from the Northeast (New York and New Hampshire).

THE PLAN OF ATTACK

Given recent economic developments, current hiring trends, and your own financial situation, you may have little choice when it comes to your first job. Chances are it will be a temporary position working in litigation in a law firm because that's where many of the jobs are right now. However, as you have seen, a paralegal career can be much more than this.

The following "plan of attack" is designed to help you determine your optimum paralegal job. Ultimately, the goal of this plan is to narrow down the choice of possible practice fields to the one that is most in tune with your interests, skills, education, and background. These five steps will help you achieve that.

Step 1: Summarize the advantages and disadvantages of each legal specialty area as you perceive them.

Step 2: Review the different types of paralegal employers.

Step 3: Clarify your career goals and objectives by answering important career-related questions.

Step 4: Take a personal inventory of your skills, interests, education, and experiences.

Step 5: Match your goals and objectives with your skills, interests, education, and experiences to determine the best direction for your paralegal job search.

(Before you look at each step in more detail, you may want to review Chapters 2 through 4. They contain information that will help you complete Step 1.)

Step 1: Summarize the Advantages and Disadvantages of Each Specialty Area

As you know by now, one of the most important factors in determining paralegal job satisfaction is the practice area you choose to work in. Since there is a difference between working in court-related specialty areas and in transactional areas, reread the discussion of specialty areas in Chapter 3. Then review the career summary boxes in Chapters 3 and 4 for each area.

Of course, this information isn't meant to be exhaustive, and it should be supplemented with information you collect on your own—including any tidbits picked up from conversations you have with working paralegals. Remember that this part of the plan of attack is purely subjective: What is an advantage to me may be a disadvantage to you. The career summaries reflect my views based on personal experiences as well as conversations with other paralegals.

Career Tip

The major difference I found between litigation and other specialty areas is that litigation centers on disputes. You're always trying to prove that you're right and/or that the other person is wrong. This gives the work an adversarial feel that simply does not exist in other practice areas. Some paralegals and attorneys thrive on this and find it stimulating; others find it stressful and draining. Be realistic about the kinds of challenges you want.

 ### *CAREER PROFILE*

From Nurse to Paralegal

"I received my bachelor's degree in nursing in 1977 and worked for six years as an operating room nurse at Harris Hospital in Fort Worth, Texas. In the summer of 1982, I read an advertisement for a nurse/legal assistant at the law firm of Darrell Keith in Fort Worth. Further inquiry led me down the road I have followed for the last several years—medical malpractice litigation. My plans are to continue in this field. I find great fulfillment combining my background as a nurse with the responsibilities of a legal assistant. Based on my experience, I recommend that any nurse who is considering a nurse/legal assistant career take one or more paralegal courses at a local college. This would provide a fundamental understanding of common legal terminology, which will assist in making the transition."—E. Earl Hauss, senior nurse/legal assistant, Fort Worth, Texas

Step 2: Review the Different Types of Paralegal Employers

Paralegal job satisfaction is also highly dependent on whether you work in a small, medium, or large law firm; corporation; government agency; or nonprofit organization. While your first position will most likely be in a law firm, the important thing to keep in mind is that there are other options available to you. To review the advantages and disadvantages of the different types of employers, refer back to the employer summaries in Chapter 2.

Step 3: Clarify Your Goals and Objectives

In most career guides, "clarify your goals and objectives" is a buzzword phrase that translates to "know thyself." The task is easier said than done! In this chapter, goals and objectives are defined in terms of the specific things that need to be considered when trying to land a job as a paralegal. The following questions will help you identify them:

1. What area of law are you most interested in—corporate, litigation, probate, real estate, patents and trademarks, estate planning, securities, administrative, or criminal?
2. Do you want to perform court-related tasks or work in a less court-oriented field, such as real estate or intellectual property?
3. Are you interested in an area that is people oriented, such as labor or immigration law?
4. Would you rather start off as a specialist in a large law firm or begin as a generalist in a small firm and decide about your specialization later on?
5. Are you interested in working in the private sector (a law firm, corporation, bank, or insurance company, for example) or in the public sector (a federal, state, or local government agency)?
6. What size law firm would you want to work in—small, medium, or large? (Remember that the larger the firm, the more resources it generally has, which is a plus. However, large firms often want their paralegals to specialize in a particular area, which can be a minus. You could be pigeonholed as someone who can do only a few things well. Small firms have fewer resources, and the paralegals who work in them often have a wide range of responsibilities.)
7. What do you want out of a paralegal position? Are you interested in it as a long-term career, as a stepping-stone to a nonparalegal career, or as a stopover on your way to law or business school? (You may not

be able to answer this question until you're actually working as a paralegal. Meanwhile, the next chapter discusses the advancement opportunities and options open to all paralegals, and it may help you for now.)

Step 4: Take a Personal Inventory of Your Skills, Interests, Education, and Experiences

After you've determined your goals and objectives regarding a paralegal career, the next step is to assess your education, skills, work experience, and, most important, your interests.

Are you fresh out of high school or college and looking to build a new career? Are you tired of your current job and considering a career change? Are you returning to the workforce after several years' absence and looking to acquire new skills?

As I related earlier, trying to figure out who you are and what you enjoy doing (in terms of work, that is) isn't easy. However, a little preplanning can help you design a more satisfying career. First, you should answer the following questions related to the kinds of skills paralegals use.

1. Do you (or would you) enjoy working independently, with minimal supervision?
2. Do you have the capability to handle several projects simultaneously without panicking? Are you able to prioritize?
3. Do you have good verbal and written communication skills?
4. Do you enjoy doing research? Are you able to find information without being told step-by-step how to locate it?
5. Are you detail oriented? Do you have good organizational skills?
6. Are you computer literate? If not, would you be willing to learn computer skills and develop them?

Next, look at your experience in other career fields, if you've worked in others. Because the paralegal field is open to anyone, the profession has become a melting pot of diverse individuals whose occupational backgrounds are quite varied. According to the National Federation of Paralegal Associations' 1995 *Paralegal Compensation and Benefits Report,* more than 75 percent of the respondents brought other occupational experiences with them to the paralegal field, predominantly that of:

Legal secretary 31%
Education 5%

Insurance 3%
Medical 3%
Accounting 3%
Court related 2%
Journalism 2%
Nursing 1%
Law enforcement 1%

In addition, upon entering the paralegal field, 23 percent of the respondents had between two and five years of experience, with 17 percent bringing ten or more years of experience to their paralegal jobs. The paralegal profession is definitely becoming a second-career option for many people.

Step 5: Match Your Goals and Objectives with Your Skills, Interests, Education, and Experiences

By matching your goals and objectives to your skills and interests, you should be able to determine the types of paralegal positions that would best suit you.

For instance, let's say you're a recent college graduate with a B.S. in chemistry, and you have worked for the past year in the research and development department of a corporation. You're bored and want to change careers. You're contemplating going to law school and believe some experience as a paralegal would help you make that decision. Your experience, skills, and education make you well suited to a job as a patent paralegal in a corporate law department.

Or perhaps you've been a nurse for the past ten years and want to change careers. You still want to use your medical knowledge and experience, if possible. A position in the area of personal injury law in a small law firm would be an excellent choice.

Suppose you're contemplating returning to the workforce after raising a family but feel that you have few marketable skills. You had some secretarial experience years ago, but you don't want to be a secretary again. You could start out as a litigation paralegal, or, if you have some computer skills, you could work in the area of computerized litigation support. As I said earlier, litigation is an excellent place to start; it can provide a basic foundation in legal procedures, and jobs are more plentiful than in other specialty areas.

Maybe you're interested in real estate and have a license, but you have found that the stress of working in sales isn't for you. You could become a paralegal in the real estate department of a law firm, corporation, or development company. That way you can stay in the field and not experience the pressure that is a part of sales.

I know someone who majored in finance, worked as a financial analyst for a few years crunching numbers, and was totally bored. She went back to school to get a paralegal certificate and is now working in securities law, specializing in mergers and acquisitions. She uses her finance background daily, and she is anything but bored.

The point is, don't discount your prior work experience, skills, or interests when looking for a job as a paralegal. You may be able to use them in a specialty area that could be very rewarding.

 C A R E E R   P R O F I L E

From Speech Therapist to Paralegal

After receiving a master's degree in speech pathology and language development, Sandy Philp spent the next twenty-five years working as a speech therapist at rehabilitation centers and hospitals. While her job was rewarding, it did have its drawbacks, namely, working on an hourly basis as an independent contractor. In 1987, after deciding that she needed a more predictable income, she enrolled in the National Center for Paralegal Training in Atlanta to obtain her paralegal certificate. After graduating, she sent out résumés and landed a job in a large Atlanta law firm. She works in both administrative and environmental law on a variety of cases involving Superfund issues, utility hearings, and health care. Her medical background has come in handy when working on hospital certification cases. She believes it was her health-care experience that proved instrumental in landing her the job. —Sandy Philp, paralegal, Atlanta

SOURCES OF EMPLOYMENT

After you've determined the best direction for your job search, the next step is to identify the employers who might hire you. Given the increase in the use of temporary paralegals and the improvement in the economy,

Methods of Obtaining Paralegal Employment	
Methods	*Percent of Paralegals Getting a Job*
Networking	25
Classified ads	19
Promotion	17
Résumé	9
Employment agency	8
School placement	5
Association job bank	4
Other	13

Source: National Federation of Paralegal Associations, Inc., 1995 *Paralegal Compensation and Benefits Report.*

chances are better than ever that you will be able to find employment. Here are some suggestions, arranged in the order that will most likely work for you.

Personal Contacts

Call it networking, call it word of mouth. There's no doubt about it—this is the best way to land a good job. It's also one of the most time consuming, especially if you don't have many contacts.

A good way to develop contacts is to join your local paralegal association. I can't tell you the number of people I have spoken to in the last few years who have not included this step in their job search, and it's a mistake.

Career Tip

I strongly advise that you join your local association while you are attending a paralegal training program and before you begin your job search. Do not wait until you are actually looking for a job. Most associations have student memberships. To find out if your area has a local paralegal association, write the National Federation of Paralegal Associations, Inc., P.O. Box 33108, Kansas City, Missouri 64114-0108, or call 816-941-4000 to obtain a list. NFPA's Website is www.paralegals.org.

These associations have a lot of valuable information and resources—including newsletters, career forums and seminars in various practice areas, and job hot lines. Most are also members of the NFPA, which publishes a quarterly newsletter that you'll receive when you join at the local level. Also, keep in mind that the legal community in most cities, even the larger ones, is relatively small and close-knit. Once you start networking, you'll get to know a lot of people in a short amount of time.

Employment Agencies and Paralegal Recruiters

Most of the nationally known employment agencies have legal divisions that recruit legal personnel. However, lacking paralegal experience themselves, many of these recruiters know little, if anything, about the field.

Within the last decade a new breed of employment agencies has emerged. For the most part, such agencies are owned and operated by former paralegals and are dedicated solely to placing paralegals. The main advantage of these agencies is that their recruiters, as former paralegals, know and understand the needs and concerns of the employer and the employee. I strongly recommend using this type of agency over the traditional kind, whose recruiters may not know a paralegal from a parakeet.

When a friend of mine was laid off after working for eight years at a large San Francisco corporation, she went to a regular agency to help her find temporary positions. Her specialty was regulatory law, and her resume showed quite clearly that she was highly skilled and experienced. She had also worked as a litigation paralegal for six years, which gave her a total of fourteen years of experience. When she interviewed for a temporary assignment, the recruiter wasn't sure if summarizing depositions (a basic skill) would be too difficult for her level of experience!

An agency owned and run by paralegals is better equipped to match a person's skills and experience with the level required for a particular position. To locate such agencies, contact your local paralegal association; it's likely to have a list of them. For a current list of paralegal recruiters nationwide, see Appendix D.

Temporary assignments. While paralegal employment agencies offer permanent and temporary placement services, temporary assignments are an excellent way to obtain your first paralegal job. They give you the opportunity to gain valuable experience and to test the waters before jumping in feet first. Temping enables you to work at several different law firms or corporations before deciding what's best for you. And organizations often offer permanent positions to temporary workers, which is what happened to Chyllene Cattie.

 CAREER PROFILE

From Temp to Permanent Paralegal

"Although I received my paralegal certificate in September 1985, I actually started working a few months before I received it. A temporary paralegal agency in Philadelphia had a position that needed someone with computer knowledge. Since I had prior experience training people on computers, they placed me in it. It involved computerized litigation for a large antitrust case. After three months, the firm realized there wasn't enough work to employ me full-time on that one case, so they began giving me other cases. Nine months later, they bought me out of my contract with the agency, and I have been here ever since."— Chyllene Cattie, paralegal, Philadelphia

Temporary assignments benefit employers as well as employees. When the economy seriously started to weaken in the early 1990s, many companies began cutting their staff to the bare bones to reduce expenses, and they have remained reluctant to increase the size of their permanent staff since then. Law firms are no different. In fact, the work that comes into law firms tends to be cyclical, which makes temporary employees an essential part of the workforce. They are hired on an as-needed basis.

Classified Ads

Many career guides advise you to stay away from the classified ads, and, for the most part, they are right. However, there are two good reasons you shouldn't discount them as a source of paralegal employment information. One, lawyers advertise to recruit clerical staff, paralegals, and attorneys all the time. Why? Because they're cost conscious and would rather advertise than pay an employment agency. And two, classified ads can be a valuable source of information, particularly when you begin your job search. You can discover all kinds of facts about employers, legal specialty areas, job duties, qualifications, and salary.

Your best source for classified ads is a legal newspaper. Jobs are usually listed by categories for attorneys, paralegals, secretaries, and office management staff. Check with your local library if you're not sure whether your area has a legal newspaper. Many paralegals have obtained jobs by answering ads in them. In fact, I have. After 3½ years as a securities paralegal in a first-rate law firm, I wanted to work in a corporation. As I went about my job search, a counselor at an employment agency told me that finding such a position would be "extremely difficult." That didn't discourage me, though. After several months, I was hired by a large corporation—a job I found by answering an ad in a San Francisco legal trade paper. Classified ads do work!

The Internet

Since the last edition of this book was published, there's a new source for obtaining career information: the Internet. While it's no substitute for the best method for getting a job, namely personal contacts, the Internet is becoming a valuable job-hunting resource for both employers and employees alike. The immediacy of the Internet gives online job seekers a foot up to those responding to traditional classified ads.

In a survey developed by Robert Half International, Inc., which appeared in the September/October 1996 issue of *Legal Assistant Today*, 61 percent of the 150 executives participating from the nation's 1,000 largest companies believed that a strong understanding of the Internet would make them more marketable in their fields.

There are several types of sites you can use to search for career information and job postings, including:

- General career information
- General circulation newspapers
- Legal newspapers
- Law firms and paralegal associations

General career information. The following is a list of some of the more popular sites that provide general career information and job listings in many fields. It is by no means exhaustive, but it is a good place to start:

CareerBuilder (www.careerbuilder.com)—Offers companies and job seekers a job-listing service and an online magazine with career advice. Users can create a résumé and respond to online ads.

Career Links (www.careertalk.com/career_links.html)—A comprehensive directory of the major career or job-listing sites.

Career Mosaic (www.careermosaic.com)—Allows you to search the JOBS database or Usenet newsgroups by keyword or topic.

E-Span (www.espan.com)—A database of over 7,000 jobs from employers who pay to be listed. It favors browsing by company rather than by searching. Also has a Special Needs section for workers with disabilities.

JobDirect (www.jobdirect.com)—A new service specializing in entry-level jobs and internships for college students and new graduates.

JobWeb (www.jobweb.org)—This site's Catapult section includes job listings by region and links to headhunters and professional associations.

Monster Board (www.monster.com)—Claims to be the most comprehensive job database on the Web, with over 55,000 job listings worldwide. The site allows you to apply to posted positions online by either copying your résumé into an e-mail message, or completing an online résumé form. Also allows you to submit your résumé to its national database, which is searched by employers who are recruiting.

Online Career Center (www.occ.com/occ)—A job-listings database searchable by industry, city, and state. Job seekers can place their résumés on line and view detailed information about member companies.

The Riley Guide (www.jobtrak.com)—Compiled by Margaret F. Riley, author of the book *The Guide to Internet Job Searching*. This site explains how to use the Internet to find a job.

General circulation newspapers. The tedium of searching through the classified ad section of your local newspaper is being replaced by the Internet. As mentioned earlier, law firms often advertise for paralegal positions in local newspapers. Most major newspapers have put their classified ads on the Internet. Here are a few of those sites:

Career Path (www.careerpath.com)—Has one of the largest online databases with over 100,000 current jobs from top newspapers around the country. According to reviews, the database is fast and easy to use; you search by region, keywords, and job descriptions. The drawback is that you're limited to only participating newspapers.

Ecola's 24-Hour Newstand (www.ecola.com/news/)—Lists sites to hundreds of daily newspapers, magazines, and computer publications from around the country (and the world). This site isn't limited to major metropolitan newspapers.

Legal newspapers. Legal newspapers are putting their classified ads online, and this is an excellent way to quickly find listings of paralegal jobs. While there are several national legal newspapers, such as *The National Law Journal* (www.lawjobs.com), that advertise paralegal jobs, the best place to find paralegal jobs in your area is from your local legal newspaper. If you do not know its Web address, call the paper to find out.

Law firms and paralegal associations. Many law firms now have their own Web pages and many more are in the process of creating them. Not only do law firms use their Web pages for e-mail, research, and communications with clients, but many also post job listings on them. In addition, your local paralegal association will most likely have a Web page and will also post job listings. This is probably one of your most direct routes to finding paralegal employment.

As was mentioned earlier, the National Federation of Paralegal Associations lists paralegal jobs on its Website at www.paralegals.org.

The Hidden Job Market

Experts say that only 20 percent of the positions in the general job market are advertised. However, due to the legal profession's propensity to use ads to recruit, I believe the percentage is higher for paralegal and other legal positions. Nevertheless, the hidden job market represents all those employers who don't advertise. It's up to the job hunter to find out who and where they are.

Luckily, this is less difficult than it may sound. If you're interested in working at a law firm, the best place to start your search is with *Martindale-Hubbell Law Directory*, the bible of the legal profession. This multivolume set of books lists the names, addresses, and telephone numbers of all lawyers and law firms in the country by state and city and is found in every law library. If you want to narrow your search down to law firms and lawyers practicing in a particular specialty area, another good source to use is your local county bar association. They usually publish a directory that lists lawyers both alphabetically and by practice area. Martindale-Hubbell is now available on CD-ROM and online at www.martindale.com.

If you want to work at a particular corporation, you'll need to get the name and title of its chief legal officer so that you can contact him or her. There are a number of directories in your local library, such as *Standard*

& Poor's Corporate Records or Dun & Bradstreet's *Million Dollar Directory*, which provide that information and other valuable facts about the company.

Obtaining a position from the hidden job market requires patience, time, and effort. During my search for a position in a corporation, I sent my résumé to the general counsels of the dozen major corporations that I had targeted with the help of the books mentioned above. I followed up with telephone calls, but, unfortunately, received no interviews. A year later, while at the job I landed through a classified ad, I received a call from the general counsel of one of those corporations. He had kept my résumé on file, and, when a job came up he thought I was suited for, he called. While I wasn't actively looking for a job at that time, he made an offer I couldn't refuse. It included a 30 percent increase in salary and the opportunity to work in new areas.

If you're pressed for time, the hidden job market may not be the best place to search for your first paralegal position. Once you have some experience and can afford the time it takes to work through the process, however, tapping into this resource will open new doors.

 CAREER PROFILE

From Housewife to Law Student to Paralegal

"At 38 years old, after raising two children, I went back to school to obtain my bachelor's degree in history. Since I had made the dean's list, I applied to and was accepted at law school. Between my first and second years, I found myself free for the summer and enrolled in the University of San Diego's eleven-week paralegal program. I thought it would help me in law school. I loved it and thought, 'Why should I spend two more years going to law school?' So in 1985, I stopped going to law school and began working as a litigation paralegal in a wonderful law firm. I've been at the same firm ever since.

"After working behind the scenes as a paralegal and seeing how unhappy some lawyers are, I'm no longer interested in going back to law school. I've found that age makes no difference. Younger lawyers seem more disillusioned because they thought it would be different. Attorneys tell me, 'You really have the best. You're not sitting on the side of your bed at two in the morning worrying if you did something

wrong the day before.' Besides, now that I'm 51, I have no desire to take time away from my husband and myself by returning to law school."— Diane Remick, senior paralegal, San Diego, California

Promotions

During the 1970s and early 1980s, it was common for legal secretaries who were already performing paralegal duties to be promoted to paralegal. This alternative route to the profession can't be overlooked. More than 31 percent of the paralegals who responded to a survey on which the NFPA's 1995 *Paralegal Compensation and Benefits Report* was based had some experience as legal secretaries before becoming paralegals. However, it's more than likely that most of the people responding to that survey began working in law firms many years ago, as did Royanne Hollins, a senior paralegal at a Sacramento, California, law firm.

"I have been working in a medium-size law firm in Sacramento, California, for the past fifteen years and began my legal career here as a green, inexperienced legal secretary," she says. "I performed many paralegal duties while maintaining my responsibilities as legal secretary. Holding down two jobs and getting paid for only one was an incentive to complete a paralegal certificate program. After graduating, I worked as a senior civil litigation paralegal where I was also in charge of paralegal staffing, hiring, and firing as well as the computerized litigation support system." Royanne was recently promoted to director of legal services and no longer performs paralegal duties. In her current position she acts as both paralegal manager and legal administrator for the firm.

Today, there are still a good many paralegals who, like Royanne, began as a legal secretary, particularly if they worked in smaller law firms. However, as stated in Chapter 5, the growing popularity of the profession and the large pool of available certified or degreed paralegals make that kind of "in" less likely.

Placement Services

Most reputable paralegal programs have placement services for new graduates and alumni. Law firms often use them to recruit new paralegals. If you're attending one of these programs or have graduated from one, be sure to check out this option.

CAREER PROFILE

"I received a bachelor's degree in accounting and worked as an accountant for two years. I was bored silly because there was not enough contact with people. Then I moved to Boulder, Colorado, and didn't know what I wanted to do, so I worked for a while as a cook in a restaurant. When a friend of mine suggested that I'd make a good paralegal, I started looking into paralegal schools. I chose the one that would give me the broadest base of knowledge. I loved it! I went two days a week while I continued to work. Part-time, the course took two years to complete.

"After the first year of school, the Manville Corporation was hiring temporary paralegals to work on a large asbestos case. I worked for it while I finished the program. While at Manville, I continued to look for a job and was hired by an insurance company's legal department. I spent two years with it doing corporate work but had the feeling that I really wanted to do litigation. I interviewed with a law firm in Denver and was really impressed with the fact that they were more concerned about whether they were right for me, not vice versa. I was hired to work in the product liability group.

"From the beginning, I knew exactly what I wanted in a paralegal position—one where I was the attorney's right hand, where I would be involved in everything, where I would be respected as part of the team."—Engrid Tronsrue, paralegal, Denver, Colorado

Internships

Internships are usually incorporated into paralegal certificate programs and offer the student an opportunity to gain on-the-job skills and experience. Many times a law firm will hire an intern after he or she has completed the program.

If you haven't graduated from a program that offers internships and you haven't had any luck landing an entry-level job, volunteering your services free for a limited amount of time can give you a leg up. If you can do it, this is the kind of experience that will help you land your first job.

Career Tip

While interning may seem like a "last-resort" strategy, it is a viable alternative in order to gain access to the field, make valuable contacts, and get paralegal work on your résumé. It is interesting to note that in fields such as marketing, advertising, radio, and TV, interning is standard practice, even in the best of economic times.

RÉSUMÉS

There are dozens of books on the market about the art of writing résumés and cover letters. However, these time-honored tools of the job search should be put in their proper perspective. In the past, the résumé was looked upon as the key to finding a job. While it is true that you cannot obtain a job without one, today more than ever it is a small component of the entire job search process.

The reality is that you'll be more apt to land your first paralegal job by attending your local paralegal association's meetings and making valuable contacts than by sitting at your computer and cranking out résumés and cover letters that might end up in someone's circular file.

While personal contacts are important, you'll eventually need a résumé that works for you, not against you. Simple rules include:

- Keep your résumé to one page. If you feel you need more space, you might attach an additional page entitled "Professional Accomplishments," where you can elaborate on your one-page résumé.

- Check and recheck for misspelled words. Spelling errors are detrimental and very unprofessional, particularly if you're applying for a position that requires excellent writing skills.

- Don't list hobbies on your résumé. This is okay for high school students applying for summer work but not for professionals.

- Don't be verbose. Keep things short and sweet. You can embellish later on in the interview. Customize your résumé and cover letters to each position. It's more time consuming but more personable.

- Be cautious when deciding whether or not to state a job objective near the top of the résumé; it may limit you.

- Don't be afraid to list jobs and activities that you may think have nothing to do with law, such as volunteer work or jobs in other careers. Often nonlegal skills acquired in these jobs can be valuable to an employer.

INTERVIEW QUESTIONS YOU NEED TO ASK

Once again, there are many books available that discuss general interviewing techniques, but none of them will contain information specifically relevant to paralegal employment.

One of the keys to paralegal job satisfaction revolves around the attitude of the employer toward paralegals. Does he or she consider paralegals professionals, or are they considered glorified clerical workers? The following questions are designed to assist you in determining your potential employer's attitude toward paralegals, which you can use to determine if you'd be happy working for such an employer.

What is the required minimum billable hours per year? Remember that all law firms require you to bill your time, and most set a minimum standard somewhere between 1,400 and 1,800 hours per year. You should ask what this translates into on a daily basis. If it's more than 6½ hours per day, you'll be working a long day because you'll need to factor in some nonbillable time for administrative matters.

Will I be paid for overtime? In other words, will you be considered a professional who is exempt from overtime, or a nonexempt employee? This hotly debated issue in the paralegal field will be discussed further in Chapter 9. Data from NFPA's 1995 *Paralegal Compensation and Benefits Report* will give you some idea of the breakdown: 51 percent of the respondents were exempt employees, 45 percent were nonexempt, and 4 percent responded "other".

What type of computer system does the firm have? This is a great indicator of the firm's attitude toward technology. As you now know, technology will play a major role not only in the type of work you will be doing but also in your job satisfaction. If the firm is still using a DOS network or (God forbid!) isn't networked at all, that's a red flag.

Does the firm have an in-house training program? Many large firms provide entry-level paralegals with some training, primarily in the area of litigation, for tasks such as legal research and deposition summaries.

Does the firm have a paralegal manager? This individual is a valuable resource in terms of directing work flow assignments and mitigating salary problems with management.

Will I have access to a secretary? If so, what type of arrangement is it? Will it be a secretarial pool, or will I share a secretary with someone? If so, with whom? The secretarial issue is important because you do not want to be doing all your own word processing.

Will I have a private office? It was reported in the 1996 salary survey in *Legal Assistant Today* that 70 percent of the respondents had private offices. A private office is important because you will need an area without distractions to perform your tasks effectively.

Does the firm have case assistants? Remember that case assistants help paralegals with the more routine tasks involving document control and organization. As I mentioned earlier, this level of legal personnel is most often used in larger law firms to assist in litigation on large cases.

Does the firm offer a senior paralegal career track? As mentioned in Chapter 2, this is offered by large law firms and is an indication of the firm's recognition of the paralegal as a professional.

Does the firm pay for continuing education seminars? Continuing education is an integral part of your paralegal career and is an important way for you to keep on top of the latest developments in your specialty area.

PARALEGAL COMPENSATION

Just what can you expect to earn as a paralegal? Given the fact that according to the NFPA's 1995 *Paralegal Compensation and Benefits Report,* paralegal salaries nationwide ranged from a low of $9,600 to a high of $125,000, with the average being roughly $32,875, this is not an easy question to answer. The huge disparity in salary ranges can be attributed to several factors, including:

- Legal specialty area
- Type of employer
- Years of experience
- Size of law firm
- Geographical region
- Local applicant pool

For instance, according to *Legal Assistant Today*'s 1996 Salary Survey, average salaries by geographical region ranged from a low of $30,166 in the Central region (including Minnesota, Wisconsin, Iowa, Missouri, Illinois, Indiana, Michigan, Kentucky, Tennessee, Alabama, Mississippi, Louisiana, and Arkansas) to a high of $38,543 in the West (including California, Nevada, Oregon, and Washington). The average salary in California was higher than any other state ($40,624). Metropolitan areas averaged $33,954, while rural averaged $27,131.

In terms of type of employer, according to the NFPA's 1995 *Paralegal Compensation and Benefits Report,* average salaries ranged from a low of $30,500 for paralegals working in city government to a high of $37,882 for those working in the federal government. Average salary by specialty area ranged from a low of $26,837 in family law, to a high of $31,571 in corporate law.

Compensation is also related to intangibles such as attorney attitude toward paralegals. Although paralegals have been a part of the legal profession for almost three decades, not every employer understands what they are and how to best use them. To some attorneys, paralegals are nothing more than document clerks, while others see them as highly skilled legal technicians who can perform a wide range of complex tasks.

Entry-level salaries. According to NFPA's 1995 *Paralegal Compensation and Benefits Report,* the ranges for base salaries for entry-level paralegals were as follows:

Under $18,000—20%
$18,001–$20,000—23%
$20,001–$22,000—17%
$22,001–$25,000—13%
$25,001–$28,000—13%
Over $28,001—14%

Maximum salaries. Just as important as what you will earn in your first one to two years is your future salary potential. The NFPA's 1995 *Paralegal Compensation and Benefits Report* states a high of $125,000 annually. Keep in mind that not many paralegals achieve six-figure incomes, although a growing number of law firms are recognizing the idea of career paralegals and are developing compensation packages that handsomely reward them. The career paralegal and specialist paralegal will be discussed in the next chapter.

Salary increases. According to *Legal Assistant Today*'s 1996 Salary Survey, the average salary increase was 6.3 percent. This did not change from the prior year's results. Approximately 14 percent of the full-time paralegals responding to the survey did not receive a raise.

Additional compensation. Some, but not all, paralegals receive bonuses and overtime pay. Bonuses were received by 62 percent of paralegals responding to the *Legal Assistant Today*'s 1996 Salary Survey, with an average dollar amount of $1,584. Most law firms pay bonuses while corporations and government agencies generally do not. According to the survey, 41 percent of paralegals were paid overtime.

Negotiating Salaries

Let's face it. Employers have the upper hand today, particularly with entry-level workers. When discussing salaries, be realistic. You're not only looking for a job, you are building a career.

One of your most important weapons is information. Before you interview, know what to expect in terms of salary. I recommend the following sources:

1. Your best bet is your local paralegal association's annual salary survey. Geographical area does make a difference in setting salaries. If by some chance your local association does not prepare a survey, you can use the next two sources, which list salaries by geographical region.
2. The National Federation of Paralegal Associations, Inc., 1995 *Paralegal Compensation and Benefits Report* is available by sending a check for $15 to the NFPA, P.O. Box 33108, Kansas City, Missouri 64114-0108. This is the first reasonably priced survey conducted by a national paralegal association.
3. *Legal Assistant Today* conducts an annual survey of its readers. The results are usually published in the January/February issue. While you might be able to obtain a back issue, I highly recommend you subscribe to this magazine. It's an excellent and informative resource not only for entry-level paralegals but also for those with experience. For subscription information, write James Publishing, Inc., P.O. Box 25202, Santa Ana, California 92799-9900, or call 800-394-2626.

You might have more bargaining power if you have something special to offer, such as a language skill or expertise in a technical area like advanced computer programming skills. And be sure to ask about bonuses because this will definitely add to your base salary. While most law firms offer bonuses, you should find out whether they are based on merit, seniority, or firm profits.

As mentioned in the section earlier in this chapter on interviewing, be sure to ask if the firm has a senior paralegal track, because salaries are usually about $5,000 to $10,000 higher for senior paralegals. Find out what the requirements are for qualifying and ask about salary and benefits.

Paralegal vs. Legal Secretary Salaries

There is a definite disparity between entry-level salaries for paralegals and those for legal secretaries. You will inevitably encounter it as soon as you begin working. For the first one to three years, legal secretaries are often paid higher than paralegals. This is primarily due to the law of supply and demand. While lawyers absolutely need legal secretaries, they can sometimes do without paralegals. After all, lawyers can do paralegal work, but how many of them can do secretarial work?

Don't be put off by this situation. Yes, secretaries are often paid more at first, but you need to consider the long-term picture. What types of tasks do you want to be doing in a job? Which career will provide you with the greatest advancement opportunities? What salary potential does a legal secretary career have to offer? Most paralegals find that within a few years' time paralegal salaries outpace those of legal secretaries.

Fringe Benefits

Benefits are part of your total compensation package. But, with the skyrocketing cost of health insurance, they are increasingly becoming an endangered species. To give you some idea of the types of benefits and the percentage of paralegals receiving them, the following statistics are taken from the 1996 salary survey in *Legal Assistant Today*:

    97%—vacation days (13.5 days per year)
    88%—health insurance and sick days (9.3 days per year)
    78%—business cards
    70%—private office
    66%—mileage
    65%—association dues
    61%—CLE (continuing legal education) course work
            reimbursement
    51%—personal days and disability insurance
    49%—dental coverage

48%—maternity leave
36%—paid parking
33%—flextime opportunities
26%—vision coverage
18%—free legal representation
14%—firm credit card and meal allowance
2%—child-care expenses
Less than 1%—"mommy" track

WHAT TO EXPECT AFTER YOU'RE HIRED

First day jitters? Definitely, particularly if you've never worked in a law firm or for a lawyer before. It's pretty normal to feel a little intimidated and overwhelmed at first, but you get over it pretty quickly. Here are a few things you might want to consider in those first few weeks.

Corporate culture. Every company has its own way of doing things, and law firms are no exception. Similar to accounting firms, they have a partnership structure that often lends itself to an us-them attitude. As a result, law firm politics are different from those of a corporation. Another difference I found is that most law firms and lawyers have a high degree of professionalism and standards that often do not exist in other professions. In terms of work product, you'll definitely find yourself having to rise to the occasion.

Billing time. This is something you'll have to get used to from day one. Remember that no one gets paid unless billable hours are accounted for. As discussed in Chapter 2, you'll have to keep track of both billable and nonbillable time. There is sometimes a tremendous amount of pressure put on paralegals and attorneys alike to bill the required number of hours.

In-house training. Depending on the size of the law firm, you might be lucky enough to have an in-house training program. During the first few weeks, you'll be doing both training assignments and your regular work. In smaller law firms where no in-house training is provided, you'll just have to take the ball and run with it. Most employers realize that it takes anywhere from six months to one year to train an employee, no matter what the job.

Ask questions. Most new paralegals are intimidated by attorneys. They are often afraid to ask questions for fear that they'll look like they don't know what they're doing. When you are given an assignment by an attorney and you either don't understand it or need clarification, definitely ask questions. The attorney may look or act annoyed, but it is better to get the assignment right the first time than to make a mistake and have to go back afterward.

Find a mentor. If the attorney is unapproachable, which oftentimes they are, your next best bet is to befriend a senior paralegal, preferably one in your practice area. This is one of the benefits to working in a large law firm where a lot of resources and people are available.

Working independently. An attorney will give you an assignment without a lot of explanation and expect you to figure out how to do it. This might come as a shock to those of you who are used to a supervisor hovering over you. As mentioned earlier in this book, common sense and the ability to locate resources will become two of your most important skills. You can expect to be working with minimal supervision right from the beginning.

Client contact. This can be one of the most interesting aspects of your job. Remember that you are not an attorney and cannot give legal advice. However, you'll probably be advising clients on factual matters. As is mentioned elsewhere in this book, don't be surprised if the client would rather talk to you than to the attorney.

Document everything. When you make an important telephone call to a client or after you complete a research assignment, you will be asked to document it in a Memorandum to File. Get used to doing this. In case a problem, question, or discrepancy comes up in the future, you'll have proof to back up what you did.

Team effort. Remember that you are part of a team consisting of attorneys, paralegals, secretaries, and other support staff whose purpose is to serve the client's needs as efficiently and effectively as possible.

Continuous education of attorneys. Even though paralegals are performing more sophisticated tasks than ever before, not all attorneys know how to use paralegals effectively. You will find that some attorneys are reluctant to delegate work. After you gain some experience and confidence, it will be up to you to educate them as to what you are capable of doing.

Some Thoughts About Working with Lawyers

If you've never worked for an attorney, there are a few things you might like to know:

- When it comes to managing people, lawyers leave something to be desired. Personnel issues are not their strong point, so don't expect too much in this department.

- Lawyers tend to work hard—very hard—and they generally want the same from all other legal personnel. Their expectations of themselves and their staff are extremely high, so be prepared. There's a lot at stake in law. After all, when things go wrong, all eyes turn to the lawyer.

- Lawyers aren't in business to win personality contests. As a result, they may not be the most personable people in the world. They're often preoccupied and in a hurry.

- Lawyers are renowned for giving vague assignments. For instance, when briefing you about the facts in a case, an attorney usually does just that—brief you. Typically, they don't have a lot of time (or patience) to stop and explain things in detail. Consequently, a lot of your learning will come by osmosis and through trial and error. (That's why you need to know how to locate information quickly and on your own.)

- Lawyers are notorious for waiting until the last minute to give you an assignment they wanted done yesterday.

- To complete an assignment on time, convert minutes to hours, hours to days, days to weeks, and so on. When a lawyer says, "This will take you only 2 hours to do," be wary! After years of hearing statements like that, I can assure you that two hours usually means 2 days.

From personal experiences, I and others in the field can testify that the ways to locate paralegal jobs described in this chapter really do work. Using the Internet, classified ads, contacting paralegal placement agencies, tapping into the "hidden" job market, and networking through your local paralegal association are effective ways to find employers who will hire you.

Once you obtain your first job and get your foot in the door, it's important to continue to make yourself as marketable as possible. With that in mind, the next chapter looks at the ways in which you can advance your career.

CHAPTER 8

Where Do You Go from Here?
Paths for Experienced Paralegals

*Success usually comes to those who are too busy
to be looking for it.*
Henry David Thoreau

■

Trust officer. Writer. Paralegal manager. Financial analyst. Pension specialist. Personnel director. Journalist. Computer sales representative. Real estate portfolio manager. Land acquisitions supervisor. Legal administrator. Law firm marketing administrator. Securities trainee. Legislative analyst. These are just some of the possibilities open to paralegals when they apply their skills and experience to other careers. Advancement opportunities are everywhere. How far you go depends on what you do with what you have. As Henry Ford once said, "Whatever you have, you must either use or lose."

In the early days of the profession, before employers recognized the potential of paralegals, the tasks and responsibilities of the job weren't very sophisticated. For many years, one of the most common complaints from working paralegals was the lack of opportunity for advancement. Overworked, underpaid, burned-out paralegals could look only to law school as a way out of what was perceived as a dead-end job. Many left the profession before the applicability of their skills to other fields became apparent.

Things are different today. The ability to specialize has provided paralegals with expanded responsibilities and opportunities for advancement inside and outside the legal field. For the most part, attorneys have recognized the value of paralegals and are using them for more and more complicated tasks. And employers outside the legal industry have seen the value of their skills, education, and training. As such, the future for paralegals with solid experience is wide open—they have the choice between remaining in the field or using it as a stepping stone to some other profession.

As you read this chapter, remember that career growth and satisfaction are subjective qualities. What is challenging and rewarding to you may be boring to someone else. A legal assistant manager for a large New York City law firm, puts it like this: "For some people, all jobs are transitional ones, representing steps in some master personal career plan. For others, any responsibility that can be defined as a job is characterized as a dead end."

THE PROBLEM WITH TITLES

Before discussing each alternative, I'd like to alert you to a problem that you might encounter at some point in your paralegal career.

The title of paralegal can pose some problems because it can be used for a number of different jobs and can represent a wide range of responsibilities. This is true in many other occupations as well. The banking industry immediately comes to mind. How many people do you know who are working in a bank with the title assistant vice president? Banks are notorious for handing out this title to almost anyone. Other than inflating the ego a bit, a title is meaningless unless it corresponds to an accurate salary range that reflects the responsibilities of the job.

I had an experience that illustrates this point. After working for four years as a corporate paralegal, I received a call from the general counsel of a large San Francisco corporation who wanted to hire me as a paralegal in a newly created position. The job sounded interesting because it combined several areas, including shareholder relations, corporate communications, and computers, with regular paralegal and legal administration duties. I was interested, but I didn't feel the title paralegal adequately represented its range of responsibilities, and I believed it would limit the salary range. The general counsel agreed. I accepted the job and was given the title legal administrator, which put my salary in a higher range than I would have received as a paralegal.

As you know by now, there is very little standardization regarding educational requirements and on-the-job responsibilities. The tasks performed by paralegals continue to increase in scope and complexity, which makes it impossible to come up with a single standardized job description.

Not having a standardized job description is a plus when it allows for a wide variety of responsibilities but a minus when it comes to trying to peg a salary to a job by its title alone. For instance, the responsibilities of a first-year litigation paralegal who spends most of the day organizing documents are quite different from those of a fifth-year probate paralegal who is specialized and an expert in a particular area. Both have the title of paralegal. Should they be paid the same? I hope not. This is a problem you will encounter when you stay within the paralegal field but start changing employers or specialty areas.

One solution would be for employers to create different titles for paralegals who become specialists in a particular practice area. For instance, I know of one large San Francisco law firm that created the title of employee benefit specialist for paralegals working in ERISA law. However, this is an exception, not the rule. It may take a number of years for paralegal employers to catch on to this idea.

CAREER TRACKS

Imagine that you've been working as a paralegal for almost three years. You feel as though you've reached the limits of your present job. You're a little bored and want a new challenge. What can you do? There are a number of alternatives. Since I've done most of them, I've arranged them in order of easiest to most difficult to accomplish, according to my experience.

1. Remain with your current employer and advance to senior paralegal or paralegal specialist
2. Stay a paralegal but change the type of employer
3. Remain a paralegal but change your legal specialty area
4. Move into paralegal management
5. Move into administration
6. Apply your paralegal skills and experience to other careers
7. Freelance and start your own business
8. Pursue additional education

Advancing to Senior Paralegal (or Paralegal Specialist)

Assuming that the law firm you're working for offers this career track, advancing to senior paralegal is perhaps the easiest of all the options to pursue. Senior paralegal status is usually found in medium-size and large law firms and in corporations with very large legal departments. It's an excellent way of rewarding experienced paralegals who are committed to a long-term career. Senior paralegals often assume some managerial and/or administrative responsibilities in addition to their ongoing paralegal duties.

Perquisites for senior paralegals usually include a higher salary scale (from $5,000 to $10,000 more than paralegals), larger bonuses, and more vacation time. Benefits to the employer include the opportunity to bill at a higher rate (which can increase profitability); it also lowers paralegal turnover, which makes for more satisfied employees. (Both of which, of course, mean greater productivity.)

Cooley, Godward, Castro, Huddleson, & Tatum, a law firm in San Francisco, recently created a new senior paralegal position called the "specialist." To qualify for the specialist position a paralegal must have twelve years experience in a particular area of expertise. The compensation package is in line with second- and third-year associate salaries, including health-club membership and access to a bonus pool. Cooley, Godward has only three specialists out of its eighty paralegals. In addition to their regular duties, they are also responsible for in-house training and mentoring. Specialists are required to bill a minimum of 1,950 hours per year. Cooley, Godward is one of a growing number of law firms nationwide that are beginning to recognize the value of retaining experienced paralegals and are willing to reward them for their efforts.

Changing Employers

After working at a large law firm for more than 3½ years, I decided I needed a change. I wanted to use my legal skills in a more generic business environment and take advantage of the benefits a corporation could offer. I landed a job in a corporate legal department. For paralegals who want to remain in the field but need a change of scenery, this track works wonders. Common moves are from large law firms to smaller ones, and from law firms to corporations.

As discussed in Chapter 2, working in a corporation has some advantages over working in a law firm. One of these may be a higher salary. For paralegals with three or more years of law firm experience who want a slower, less hectic pace, corporations are the answer. Also, if you're thinking about going back to school part-time, most corporations offer some kind of tuition reimbursement plan. But working in a corporation has its disadvantages, too. There may be less job security. With the current corporate downsizings and restructurings, you could wake up one morning and find out that you no longer have a job.

Changing Legal Specialty Areas

This alternative takes a bit more effort than changing employers. But my own experience left me believing that such a change is well worth that effort. As I said earlier, after only a year in litigation I just wasn't satisfied—even though I was working for great attorneys on cases that were quite interesting. Three months after telling the paralegal manager of the firm that I wanted to move out of litigation, I moved into the corporate and securities group. I knew immediately that I had done the right thing. My new responsibilities included the securities filings of small, start-up, high-tech companies. Since the job required that I be in touch with the Securities and Exchange Commission (SEC), underwriters, and investment bankers, it was a great way to learn about the securities industry.

Finding another position with the same law firm is only one way to change legal specialty areas. Other routes include changing firms and taking courses or continuing education seminars in the area of interest.

Moving into Paralegal Management

In 1979, a friend of mine was hired by a small law firm in Hartford, Connecticut, as its first paralegal. As the firm added more attorneys and paralegals, she assumed additional responsibilities, including the coordination and supervision of six other paralegals. Today, she coordinates the firm's entire paralegal program and manages more than twenty-five paralegals. By taking on additional duties, she was able to carve out a niche that provided her with a way into management.

Paralegal management is a traditional career move for experienced paralegals. Depending on the size of the firm, some paralegal managers split their time between managerial duties and paralegal duties, while others function solely as managers. Responsibilities include interviewing and recruiting paralegals; coordinating projects and assignments between paralegals; designing, implementing, and maintaining in-house training programs; administering salaries; and evaluating performance. Paralegal managers also function as liaisons between paralegals and other levels of management. This is a delicate role, particularly for managers who continue to perform their regular paralegal duties. In addition, salaries for paralegal managers are significantly higher than the salaries for senior paralegals.

Laurie Roselle, paralegal coordinator at a New York City law firm, enjoys the dual role. "I did it on purpose because I firmly believe that you cannot supervise people when you don't know what those people are doing. When I first started working here, the firm was strictly looking for a paralegal supervisor. I told them I didn't want to lose my paralegal skills, and so we worked out an agreement. When work comes in, I reserve the right to handle it, but I am also responsible for the hiring, firing, and training of over twenty paralegals."

If you're considering this option, check out potential employers carefully. Not every law firm or corporation has a paralegal management career track.

Moving into Administration

Administration is considered by some to be an excellent avenue for career advancement. The two positions commonly associated with this path are legal administrator and law firm marketing administrator.

Legal administrator. Legal administration was formally recognized as a career within the legal industry in 1971, with the inception of the Association of Legal Administrators (ALA). Before that, law office management was delegated to lawyers who often had little interest in administrative matters. Since the competition for clients has heated up and profitability is a real concern for law firms, the role of the legal administrator has become critical to the business side of law. "Legal administrators are the management generalists in an organization full of specialists," states former ALA President Beverlee Johnson. "Our role—planning, integrating, evaluating, motivating—provides the glue that holds the organization's processes and players together."

More than 90 percent of legal administrators work in law firms, 5 percent work in corporate legal departments, and less than 2 percent work in government agencies. A legal administrator manages the planning, marketing, business functions, and operations of a law office. Responsibilities include finance, human resources, computer systems, and facilities planning. A legal administrator might also be involved in other areas of law firm management, including policymaking, business development, attorney recruitment, and legal services marketing. Since legal administration is a managerial career track, the average salary is substantially higher than the average salary for paralegals and paralegal managers.

Legal administrators may be attorneys who are more interested in managing than in practicing law, paralegals or paralegal managers who have taken on additional administrative duties, or professional managers with no legal experience who are recruited because of their expertise in finance, personnel, data processing, marketing, or other business support areas. Because they understand the nature of law firms and the needs of lawyers and clients firsthand, paralegals have an edge in winning these jobs over managers with no legal background. Also, since monitoring a firm's profitability is an important area of legal administration, a paralegal's understanding of billing and tracking time is extremely valuable.

Law firm marketing administrator. This is a new career niche that has emerged in the past few years. Since the rules that govern the use of advertising by lawyers were relaxed by the courts over a decade ago, lawyers have begun to realize the benefits of marketing and advertising their services. Since competition for clients is keen, the marketing administrator plays a vital role in client development and in a firm's profitability.

Susan Roe, paralegal coordinator at a San Francisco law firm, is a paralegal manager who moved into marketing administration by assuming responsibilities in that area. "I started as paralegal coordinator for a law firm that never had one," she admits. "After one year, the partners began to give me other responsibilities such as preparing the newsletter and coordinating the firm's anniversary party. It just happened. Once I had a base, I started building on it. In addition to overseeing the in-house paralegal program, I am responsible for the marketing and recruiting functions of the firm.

"On the marketing side, I prepare the firm's monthly newsletter and brochures as well as coordinate all client development activities and social events. I am also responsible for recruiting on college campuses, which begins in September of each year. You always have to come up with different ways of advertising your services. For instance, I got the idea to have the slogan 'Just Say No to Drugs' and 'Gordon & Rees' imprinted on the trash bags you use in your car. We passed them out everywhere, and the response we received was phenomenal.

"For anyone interested in getting into marketing administration, the easiest way is to get your foot in the door as a paralegal or paralegal manager. Once you have a solid position, you can build on it by assuming marketing responsibilities," Susan concludes.

While some marketing administrators are recruited from the outside—particularly in large firms—in small firms, paralegals often have an advantage over these individuals (as Susan did) when it comes to this position.

For more information on this career, contact the National Law Firm Marketing Association at 60 Revere Drive, Suite 500, Northbrook, Illinois 60062, or call 847-480-9641.

Career Tip

In smaller law firms, some of the advancement opportunities mentioned so far are often combined into one job. A common example of this is a paralegal who is promoted into a position that includes both paralegal management and legal administration responsibilities. This was the case for Royanne Hollins, whose story is in Chapter 7. She moved from legal secretary to paralegal to director of legal services for a sixteen-attorney Sacramento, California, law firm and is a good example of a paralegal who took advantage of promotional opportunities.

Applying Paralegal Skills to Other Careers

Paralegals have an advantage over other paraprofessionals. Unlike a paramedic, whose skills can be used only in the medical field, a paralegal can use his or her knowledge and skills outside of a law firm or corporate law department in a number of legal- and nonlegal-related occupations. The following career paths are just some examples of the advancement opportunities open to paralegals. The first five careers—recruitment, sales, teaching, writing, and government jobs—are applicable to all paralegals, no matter what specialty area they work in. The remaining careers require expertise in a particular practice area.

Recruitment. Temporary employment agencies are among the fastest-growing industries today. As discussed in Chapter 7, agencies dedicated solely to the placement of paralegals are a recent phenomenon, and positions within these agencies represent excellent alternatives for paralegals. These agencies differ from traditional employment agencies in that they are usually run by former paralegals who not only understand the paralegal field but also the needs and requirements of law firms. Some ambitious paralegals are finding employment in these agencies, and they are also starting out on their own.

Denise Templeton is one paralegal who made the transition into the recruitment field. In 1983, she founded the first paralegal employment firm, Templeton & Associates, in Minneapolis, Minnesota. "I thought it would be a good idea to start a temporary paralegal agency that would provide law firms with experienced paralegals rather than those at the entry level," she says. "While we place both permanent and temporary paralegals, most assignments are in the area of litigation, since that's where the biggest need is. We've grown 20 percent per year. Within the past few years, we've opened new offices in Chicago and San Francisco. In addition, we've added a legal secretaries division and now offer computerized deposition summary services."

Sales. A career path often overlooked by many paralegals is sales. Besides computer hardware and software products, there are many other services that can be marketed to the legal industry—legal publication sales and photocopy services, for instance. Companies such as Matthew Bender, WESTLAW, and BNA (Bureau of National Affairs) publish books, reports, and updates that are vital to every law library. Companies like these are almost always looking for competent sales representatives who understand the legal industry. Paralegals obviously have an edge over salespeople who don't have legal backgrounds and often don't understand the legal profession. (Keep in mind that most sales positions are based on commissions, which means that what you earn depends on how much you sell.)

Teaching. Paralegal program administrators are always looking for qualified paralegals to teach a course or two. If you have several years of experience in a particular area and are interested in teaching, you should contact the programs in your area. Although schools often use attorneys to teach paralegal classes, students commonly complain that lawyers focus more on theory than practical skills. Instructors who are paralegals have firsthand experience in the day-to-day realities of the job.

Teaching is an excellent way to increase your professional status and to supplement your income. Most teaching positions are part-time, but with some classroom experience you could work your way into a full-time position as program coordinator or administrator.

Diane Remick, senior paralegal at a San Diego law firm, is an instructor in the University of San Diego's paralegal program. "I started teaching as a result of my position as secretary for the San Diego Association of Legal Assistants. This is my second year teaching. Once you get your class organized and outline prepared, it's enjoyable. I become a different person behind a podium—it's a high. I teach Introduction to Legal Systems two quarters a year. The course is an introduction to everything—civil procedure, legal research, and six other areas of law. Teaching part-time while working full-time gives me the best of both worlds," she explains. "Also, teaching has led to advisory board work for the University of San Diego and the San Diego Community College District, as well as a position on the ABA-accreditation team for paralegal education."

Diane Petropulos, who started her paralegal career in 1974, took teaching one step further. In 1983, she assumed directorship of Sonoma State University's Attorney Assistant Program. This is somewhat unusual since very few of the 800 or so paralegal programs in the United States are run by paralegals. Most are headed up by either attorneys or educators. As a former paralegal, Diane brings with her the practical knowledge that is often lacking in programs run and staffed exclusively by attorneys.

Writing. Since paralegals spend most of their time developing writing and research skills, nonfiction writing is a natural career alternative for paralegals, as my own experience demonstrates.

Most nonfiction writers start their careers by getting a few articles published before attempting to write a book. Not so with me. My only published works before I wrote the first edition of this book consisted of one travel article and a letter to the editor of a Bay Area newspaper about the 1988 presidential campaign—not exactly an impressive list of credentials! But I knew I could write, and I knew I had something to say that hadn't been said before. It was just a matter of convincing a publisher.

However, I don't recommend launching a writing career with a book. Paralegals who are interested in pursuing such a career might begin by writing an article for either a lawyer or paralegal trade journal on some aspect of the field. Paralegal journals such as *Legal Assistant Today* and the *Journal of Paralegal Education and Practice* are excellent places to begin. Once you get a few articles published, you will have developed a portfolio of writing samples, which could help you land writing jobs in other areas, including journalism, business writing, and technical writing.

I recommend subscribing to *Writer's Digest*, which offers valuable information on how to get into the business. Another helpful tool is *Writer's Market*, a book that lists the names and addresses of publishers alphabetically and by the subject matter they publish. It was through *Writer's Market* that I found Peterson's for this book.

Leanne Cazares, executive editor of *Legal Assistant Today*, is a former paralegal who ventured into the world of publishing. After earning a bachelor's degree in sociology from the University of California, Santa Barbara, in 1982, and a paralegal certificate from the University of West Los Angeles in 1984, Leanne worked for the next two years as a paralegal in the Los Angeles District Attorney's office. After a brief stint at law school in San Diego, Leanne returned to the paralegal field. She worked in San Diego law firms in litigation and labor law.

Needing a change, she decided to apply her paralegal skills to an alternative career and landed a job as an editor at *Legal Assistant Today*. She spent the next year editing a line of attorney books before she took over the magazine as editor.

Government jobs. The federal government employs more than 300,000 people in law-related positions, more than twice the number of employees since I wrote the second edition of this book in 1992. There is estimated to be approximately 140 U.S. government law-related careers, for which a paralegal certificate is not required but is considered an asset. In fact, the U.S. Office of Personnel Management reports that the number of paralegals in the federal government has increased over 30 percent during the last decade. The following is a list of just some of the jobs in government for which you could be hired if you have experience in particular legal specialty areas:

Position	*Legal Specialty Area*
Mediation specialist	Labor
Labor/management relations examiner	
Criminal investigator	Litigation (criminal)
Clerk of the court	
Realty specialist	Real estate
Land law examiner	
Patent adviser	Intellectual property
Copyright examiner	
Tax law specialist	Tax
Internal revenue officer	
Estate tax examiner	
Estate planning/probate	

Other law-related jobs in government include equal opportunity specialist, employee relations specialist, labor relations specialist, civil rights analyst, contract administrator, immigration inspector, hearings and appeal officer, legislative analyst, insurance examiner, intelligence analyst, foreign affairs officer, foreign law specialist, international trade specialist, technical information specialist, social insurance administrator, public utilities specialist, and social service representative. Many of these are mid- or senior-level positions.

As of early 1997, mid-level positions (grades GS-9 through GS-12) ranged in salary from the low 30s to the high 50s, and senior positions (grades GS-13 through GS-15) ranged from the low 50s to the high 90s . For more information on government jobs, I highly recommend contacting Federal Reports, Inc., which publishes a helpful book entitled *The Paralegal's Guide to U.S. Government Jobs: How to Land a Job in 140 Law-Related Areas,* in Washington, D.C., at 202-393-3311. The cost is $19.95 per copy for individuals and $26.95 for institutions.

Computer specialist. The world of technology and computers is wide open to paralegals who are computer literate—particularly those who have gone beyond the basics and learned programming languages. The combination of paralegal and computer skills is unbeatable. For instance, when I was a legal administrator, I was responsible for finding and purchasing a stock option software package that could be used on the firm's microcomputer. (We had been paying a large monthly fee to a time-share company through which the data were accessed via a modem.) Since I had over four years of experience in stock options and computers, I knew exactly what was needed. When one of the vendors demonstrated a product, I offered some suggestions about how it could be improved. To my surprise, the next day the company's vice president called to offer me a position as West Coast sales representative. I turned the job down, but it just goes to show how far expertise can take you!

Opportunities for paralegals in the computer industry exist in consulting firms, software firms, computer hardware companies, and companies that provide litigation support services.

Eva DeNegri is an example of a paralegal who made the successful transition into legal technology. Eva was working as a labor and employment paralegal at Morrison & Foerster in San Francisco for ten years when Lawgic Publishing Company, a start-up legal software company, recruited her to become an associate product developer. Lawgic develops expert systems software to help attorneys draft documents in employment, business, corporate, and family law. Lawgic was one of Morrison's clients, and Eva had been working with Lawgic to help them update their software products in employment law.

Since Lawgic knew her work and needed someone to assist the vice president of product development, Eva was the logical choice. As an associate developer, Eva assists product development in building and updating its products. One of her primary responsibilities is to use Lawgic's proprietary authoring tool to modify the legal analysis and table of authorities for each product.

Legal industry consulting, particularly in the area of computers and automation, is a growing opportunity for paralegals who are computer literate. Many of the large national accounting firms have legal divisions that offer consulting services to law firms. Browsing through the *New York Times* recently, I noticed an ad for one of these firms that read:

Litigation Support Consultant

We are seeking a senior consultant to join the staff of our New York Legal Services Group. This individual will have three years of experience working for a litigation support vendor or for a law firm as a litigation paralegal. Excellent oral and written communication skills and experience with microcomputer software packages are required. A bachelor's degree in English is desirable.

Paralegals can also work as consultants for computer companies such as IBM, Hewlett-Packard, and Digital, which market hardware products. Another career alternative in this area is selling for a company that specializes in legal software applications. Today there are literally hundreds of computer companies that produce software for litigation support, document management, database services, accounting and billing, docket control, and word processing, as well as for specialty practice areas such as tax, probate, and corporate law. Each one of these companies represents a potential opportunity for paralegals who are computer literate.

An option for paralegals with several years' experience in computerized litigation systems is a position with a litigation support company. These companies are often hired by law firms that do not have the resources to handle litigation support in-house.

Another interesting alternative is to work for companies that produce sophisticated computer graphics and animation. As Chapter 6 pointed out, computer graphics is becoming an important tool in the courtroom. These companies are hiring more and more paralegals.

Corporate secretary. For paralegals with experience in corporate law, pursuing a position as corporate secretary is a natural choice for career advancement. The corporate secretary is an officer-level position within a corporation that can be filled by a lawyer or a nonlawyer.

After working for four years as a corporate and securities paralegal, I was hired by a large corporation to take on the duties of the corporate secretary. The responsibilities included preparing for board of directors and shareholder meetings, managing shareholder relations programs, administering dividend reinvestment and stock option plans, managing proxy solicitation, preparing securities filings, and monitoring insider-trading compliance.

Compensation for corporate secretaries varies greatly, depending on the size of the organization, the size of the staff, the geographic location, the title of the position, and the educational background of the individual. In a 1995 survey conducted by the American Society of Corporate Secretaries, the average salary range was between $60,000 and $120,000. This range may reflect the fact that approximately 60 percent of all corporate secretaries are attorneys. Many nonlawyers begin this career track as an assistant corporate secretary. While the job market is small and competition is fierce, this can still be an excellent career goal.

For more information on such positions, contact the American Society of Corporate Secretaries, Inc., 521 Fifth Avenue, New York, New York 10175, or call 212-681-2000.

Shareholder/investor relations and corporate communications. For paralegals with experience in securities law, shareholder relations is a natural career alternative. As I said earlier, one of my responsibilities as a legal administrator was administration of the company's shareholder relations program. This included monitoring the shareholder base of the company, tracking the number of shares in all stock plans, supervising the stock transfer agent, managing the proxy solicitation process, filing various securities reports, and handling all shareholder communications.

All or part of these duties can also be handled by a corporate communications manager or an investor relations manager. These are two other possible career tracks for paralegals with experience in the corporate and securities areas. Depending on the size of the company, corporate communications and investor relations are either combined into one department or are two separate functions. Individuals in these positions are responsible for all of a company's internal and external communications, including the annual report, press releases, employee newsletters, executive video presentations, and communications with investment community personnel such as securities analysts, brokers, and portfolio managers.

Many individuals who enter the investor relations field, in particular, are seasoned professionals with accounting, finance, or operations backgrounds or with experience in the securities industry. As a result, this is a difficult field for paralegals to enter.

For more information on the investor relations field, contact the National Investor Relations Institute, 8045 Leesburg Pike, Suite 600, Vienna, Virginia 22182, or call 703-506-3570. You can visit the Institute's Web site at www.niri.org.

Court administration. Court administration involves a combination of managerial, administrative, and paralegal duties and is an excellent career move for litigation paralegals who have several years of experience. Since these positions are located in federal, state, and local government agencies, hiring procedures follow stricter guidelines than in the private sector. Responsibilities include the areas of calendar management, case flow procedures, personnel studies, facilities planning, and automation needs assessment.

Investigation. Private investigation is an interesting but somewhat offbeat area that uses many of the research skills acquired by paralegals. When Julie Champion finished her paralegal certificate program, she realized that she enjoyed the research component of paralegal work best. Instead of seeking work in a traditional paralegal capacity, she applied for a position as a private investigator in Sacramento, California.

"I always liked to figure out puzzles. I could pick up a mystery novel, start reading it, and know the answer in a few minutes," she says. "I thought the paralegal field would be interesting because I like to read and do research. But after attending paralegal school, I found I didn't like the paperwork aspect of it. So I took the research and investigative part of paralegal work and applied for positions in the area of private investigation. While most investigators had a law enforcement background, I did not. What I did have was a strong desire to learn and good research skills. I would not take 'no' for an answer, and I was hired as a trainee," she explains.

Julie's job entailed 50 percent workers' compensation and personal injury cases and 50 percent homicide cases. Her duties involved meeting with claims adjusters, contacting all the parties involved in a claim, gathering background information and witness statements, preparing reports, taking photographs, and doing surveillance work. She also supervised the investigators and the secretarial staff and was the office administrator.

According to Julie, most of her clients were insurance companies and law firms that specialized in workers' compensation and personal injury cases. "Contrary to popular belief," she offers, "we had very few clients who wanted their husband or wife investigated."

She reports that most investigators work on a contract basis per case and receive anywhere from $10 to $25 per hour and up, depending on the case and type of service. A full-time in-house investigator (usually a former police officer) who works for a law firm can earn $70,000 to $80,000 per year. "I definitely see myself staying in the field of investigation," says Julie. "I feel I have a lot more options available to me because of my paralegal degree and investigative background."

Arbitration and mediation. As mentioned in Chapter 1, paralegals who have experience in labor law and labor relations might want to consider a position in arbitration as an alternative career. Arbitration is fast becoming a major way of settling disputes in areas such as labor/management relations, commercial transactions, and, more recently, uninsured motorist and no-fault insurance plans.

In arbitration, each party presents oral testimony and relevant documents, and sometimes witnesses are called at a hearing conducted by an arbitrator. The arbitrator is an impartial person chosen by the parties involved in the dispute and is vested with the power to make the decision, which is binding on both parties, that will resolve the dispute.

You should be aware, however, that the majority of arbitrators are attorneys. As a result, it may be more difficult for paralegals not only to pursue a career in arbitration but also to establish credibility in the area. An alternative career to arbitration might be mediation, which is a less formal, nonbinding method of dispute resolution.

Freelancing and Starting a Business

"Being a freelance paralegal is the culmination of whatever legal talent I have. My income exceeds any salary I could ever earn as an employee of a law firm," says Linda Harrington, president of Linda Harrington Associates in San Francisco. "The freelance aspect of our profession is growing. I hear of paralegals in many cities setting up their own businesses. When the attorneys realize the economic benefits to them, freelancing will be an arrangement suggested by them, not merely accepted by them."

Ms. Harrington is one of the paralegal profession's success stories. She spent over seven years in several different law firms, gaining experience in the areas of probate, bankruptcy, civil litigation, domestic relations, and personal injury law. In 1973, she decided to strike out on her own and began her business by offering freelance probate services from her house with the aid of an answering service and typewriter. That was quite an accomplishment if you consider that during the early 1970s many lawyers had never even heard of a paralegal, let alone a freelance paralegal. The services offered by her company include the preparation of tax returns, accountings, inventories, and other court documents. All of the work performed by her staff is reviewed by attorneys.

She has some sound advice about freelancing: "Choose an area where there's money to be made. For example, personal injury is not a good specialty area because most lawyers work on contingency. On the other hand, the probate area is almost guaranteed money because there isn't a winner or loser. Your fee is based on a percentage of the estate. What scares me the most are the people who come out of paralegal programs and have never worked in a law firm environment. Their main reason for becoming a paralegal is to start their own business. When they get out there, they realize they do not have the experience; they're not prepared."

Not all freelance paralegals operate businesses like Linda Harrington does. Many are sole proprietors who work out of their homes and make just enough money to live on.

How to start a freelance paralegal business. For each paralegal, the path to freelancing is slightly different. Linda Harrington began to freelance while working as a full-time paralegal. I began freelancing for the company where I had been working when it announced plans to relocate farther away than I wanted to commute. After quitting as a full-time employee, I contracted for several months with the legal department until the relocation was complete. Other freelance assignments came to me by word of mouth.

At some point in our careers, most of us dream of owning our own business. In the 1980s, it seemed like everyone wanted to be an entrepreneur. But as we all know, it's easier said than done. According to the Small Business Administration, 90 percent of all businesses fail within the first three years, which is not an encouraging statistic. Before you decide to strike out on your own, consider the following:

1. *Don't quit your present position.* The safest and most conservative approach is to do work on the side while retaining your full-time position. When the extra work begins to interfere with your full-time job, it may be time to devote all your efforts to your new business.
2. *Cultivate your contacts.* Any freelance paralegal will tell you that networking and word-of-mouth referrals are vital to a successful business. Local paralegal and attorney associations are excellent places to advertise your services.

3. *Sell a specialty.* Part of Linda Harrington's success is due to her expertise in a particular practice area. In addition to probate, other promising freelance areas include litigation, computerized litigation support services, and corporate law. Litigation and computerized litigation support are probably the most popular services offered by freelancers. Typical jobs include summarizing depositions, preparing for trial, drafting pleadings, interviewing clients, cite checking, locating witnesses, researching facts, and managing computerized litigation support systems. A paralegal with experience in corporate law could offer incorporation services.

4. *Minimize your start-up costs.* Should you rent office space, or should you start the business out of your own home? If you decide to work out of an office, don't go out and purchase the most expensive office furniture, computer, or phone systems. Keep overhead to a minimum, and it will be easier to show a profit.

Career Tip

A word of warning about freelancing. I've spoken to many people interested in a paralegal career who intend to start freelancing immediately after receiving their paralegal certificate. I'd advise against this. Freelancing is not for the novice paralegal. For one, you need to gain experience in the law firm environment working with attorneys. They do have their quirks. Also, since word-of-mouth is the best way to get clients, it will be difficult for you to do so without references.

Independent contractor or employee? A question that has come up in my own experience as a freelance paralegal is whether I was an independent contractor or an employee. The answer has important ramifications for both the paralegal and the employer. As an independent contractor, you're allowed to operate as a sole proprietor and take certain business deductions on state and federal income taxes. Employees can't take those deductions.

One of the most important guidelines for determining the difference between an independent contractor and an employee involves the issue of who controls the work performed. An independent contractual relationship can be assumed when an employer receives the final product and is not involved in the methods used to perform the work. This is a difficult criterion to meet for paralegals whose job by definition entails performing work under the supervision of an attorney. However, experienced paralegals will tell you that the phrase "under the supervision of an attorney" is loosely followed; attorneys don't always have the time to review a paralegal's work.

Freelance vs. independent paralegal. It's important to understand the distinction between an independent paralegal and a freelance paralegal. A freelancer is someone who offers services to attorneys and works under their supervision. Independent paralegal is a title coined by Ralph Warner, cofounder of Nolo Press and the self-help law movement, to describe a nonlawyer who offers services directly to the public and does not work under the supervision of an attorney. As I said earlier, most states consider this in violation of the unauthorized practice of law statutes. As you'll see in the next chapter, there is some disagreement as to what constitutes practicing law.

Pursuing Additional Education

This is a traditional method for switching careers and one that should be considered by paralegals. But it's difficult because it often involves a combination of putting out extra energy, giving up time, and juggling finances.

Law school. A discussion of career alternatives wouldn't be complete without mentioning the so-called road to riches—law school. There are many misconceptions surrounding law school. My experiences have led me to discover that:

- Contrary to popular belief, attending law school does not automatically mean you'll earn a six-figure income. Also, not every attorney who works for a law firm eventually becomes a partner
- Unlike other graduate degree programs that weigh work background and personal experience for admission, law schools place a great deal of emphasis on two figures: undergraduate grade point average and Law School Admission Test (LSAT) scores. If your GPA is average and/or if you are not a good test taker, getting into a good law school will be difficult
- Most law firms, no matter how large or small, want the best lawyers. Therefore, most recruit the top law students from the top schools in the country
- Only the top law school graduates will receive starting salaries of $70,000–$85,000 per year

- Many experienced paralegals earn just as much as lawyers who have graduated from less competitive law schools

- Many people attend law school because they just don't know what else to do. That's the wrong reason to become a lawyer

- In weak moments, some lawyers will admit that practicing law is not what they thought it would be

- Paralegals are probably the most qualified individuals to make a decision about attending law school

From what I've seen, I sincerely believe there are easier ways to make a living than being a lawyer. An attorney I worked for once remarked, "If I had to do it over again, I'd become either an investment banker or an orthodontist—less work for more money."

If you're considering law school, you might want to read Ralph Warner's *29 Reasons Not to Go to Law School*. As he puts it, "This book can save you three years, $30,000, and your sanity."

There are, however, two sides to every coin. Mary Hitt was a paralegal for many years and a president of the NFPA before she decided to become an attorney. "I was a tax paralegal for a long time and was very involved in the field," she says. "I did everything I could to advance myself as a paralegal. I received a master's degree in tax and was an enrolled IRS agent, which allowed me to represent clients at IRS and administrative hearings. However, after all these things I still wasn't getting the responsibility I wanted. Instead they gave the work to a recent law school graduate who clearly didn't know half of what I knew. I finally realized that if I wanted to assume more responsibility, I had to go and get the piece of paper.

"The major difference between being a paralegal and being an attorney is that attorneys have a lot more responsibility. They are actually making the decision for their clients and interpreting the law. They get the hassles, and they get the rewards," concludes Mary.

The question you have to ask yourself when considering a law degree is how much responsibility you want out of a job and a career. Clearly, Mary went to law school for the right reasons. She had reached the limit of her responsibilities as a paralegal but was interested enough in the area to want to assume a higher level of responsibility.

Another alternative, of course, would be to attend law school to obtain a degree but not pursue a career as a lawyer. I know someone who didn't pass the California bar (actually, I know many people who didn't pass the bar) who is now selling commercial real estate. The only reason he was hired over other applicants was that he had a Doctor of Jurisprudence degree.

Other education alternatives. One of the first attorneys I worked for advised me to get an MBA and not bother with a law degree because, according to him, "You can do more with an MBA." An MBA was to the 1980s what a law degree was to the 1970s. It seemed everyone was getting an MBA and heading for Wall Street. Then came the October 1987 stock market crash and the insider-trading scandals. Jobs were lost, and the MBA was seen in a more realistic light.

For paralegals interested in moving into management, an MBA is still a good bet. You don't have to go to the best business school in the country to get a great job. In addition, you can attend business school at night while working full-time. Just try to do this with law school—I know someone who did, and she has yet to recover from the experience.

Besides getting an MBA, there are other education alternatives to pursue. For instance, a tax paralegal might do course work in accounting to earn a CPA license. Corporate and securities paralegals could take courses to earn a certified financial planner (CFP) license. By the same token, a real estate paralegal might want to obtain a real estate license.

No matter which option you choose—from staying in your present position to pursuing additional education—you need to take an active role in shaping your career. Opportunity comes in many disguises.

The next chapter discusses licensing, certification, and other issues that are critical to the future of the paralegal profession. Because these matters will affect every paralegal's job, they are too important—and too controversial—to be ignored.

CHAPTER 9

Cutting-Edge Issues Affecting Your Paralegal Career

*The world hates change, yet it is the only thing
that has brought progress.*
Charles F. Kettering

■

In Nashville, Tennessee, a paralegal opens a document preparation business called Paralegal Centers of America that handles uncontested divorces for a modest fee.

In New Jersey, a paralegal offers her services on a freelance basis to a small law firm that cannot afford to hire a full-time, permanent paralegal. All of her work is performed under the supervision of an attorney.

In New York, a paralegal prepares the closing documents for a commonplace residential real estate transaction.

What do these individuals all have in common? According to some legal experts they are all practicing law and are in violation of what is known as the unauthorized practice of law (UPL) statutes. These are the laws, court rules, and bar association powers dating back to the 1930s that prohibit nonlawyers from providing legal services directly to the public. The unauthorized practice of law is one of the most controversial issues facing paralegals today and certainly one that you will encounter in your paralegal career.

If you're contemplating a career as a paralegal, it's important to understand this issue as well as others that concern the profession, including certification, education standards, the status of paralegals as nonexempt employees under U.S. labor laws, and the underutilization of paralegals.

The controversy surrounding paralegals is a clear indication that it is time to reassess the roles of attorneys and paralegals, especially in terms of the goal to make high-quality, cost-effective legal services available to everyone. Such a reassessment could also benefit paralegals by expanding their responsibilities. This kind of reassessment will also help the paralegal profession achieve its own goal of broadening paralegal job responsibilities.

ISSUE: UNAUTHORIZED PRACTICE OF LAW

Just what is considered "practicing law"? This is hard to determine because there is no uniform definition of just what exactly constitutes the practice of law.

The UPL statutes raise some hotly debated questions. Why should lawyers have a monopoly on every aspect of the delivery of legal services—including the right to fill in the blanks on preprinted divorce forms? What's wrong with nonlawyers providing routine and basic legal services directly to the public? Why can't we have several different levels of legal professionals who could offer varying degrees of legal services at competitive rates?

In the state of New York only a lawyer can handle real estate closings, but in California a nonlawyer can perform the same tasks without being in violation of UPL. Professionals such as bankers and accountants prepare and file documents that can be considered legal in nature. Are they practicing law? What about the proliferation of self-help books and software for preparing simple wills, bankruptcies, and other legal documents? If you have used these books and software programs to prepare a will for someone else, are you practicing law?

There were many times during my tenure as a paralegal when I exercised independent judgment, made decisions based on that judgment, and then prepared and filed the corresponding documents without having them reviewed by an attorney. Under the strictest definition, I could have been in violation of UPL. In theory, all paralegals should be supervised by the attorneys who are ultimately responsible for their work; in reality there are many times when this supervision just does not happen.

Defining the Problem

The UPL issue of unauthorized practice of law revolves around two separate concerns: (1) the inability of the legal profession to provide all citizens access to high-quality, cost-effective legal services and (2) the difficulty of redefining and expanding the roles and responsibilities of nonlawyers, including paralegals, in order to meet the legal needs of all citizens.

Access to legal services. In 1975, James D. Fellers, then president of the American Bar Association, described the bar's most important mission as beginning a push to "bring legal assistance to every American, not just those privileged enough to be able to pay for it or those impoverished enough to be eligible for free legal aid." Fellers put his finger on a basic problem in our society—middle-income people who need basic legal services for divorces, incorporations, name changes, wills, adoptions, or bankruptcy are not rich enough to pay for high-priced attorneys and not poor enough to qualify for legal aid.

The legal industry responded to this prodding by introducing prepaid legal insurance plans, group legal services, and lawyer referral services; lifting prohibitions on advertising by lawyers; and hiring more paralegals and making better use of them. But many paralegal and consumer groups and some attorneys believe that more needs to be done. Looking for ways to lower the cost of basic legal services, these groups believe that properly educated and trained nonlawyers can provide basic services at lower rates than licensed attorneys.

Among the people who object to allowing nonlawyers to provide such services are lawyers who work either as sole practitioners or in small law firms. This group of lawyers represents over half of all attorneys in private practice and has the most to lose from direct competition. Attorneys who work in large firms don't have as much to lose because large firms make money from complex legal transactions and not from simple wills, incorporations, or bankruptcies.

Perhaps now you can begin to see the dilemma. Lawyers are ethically bound to provide all citizens with access to legal services, but, because of the cost of those services, not all citizens can afford a lawyer when they need one.

In 1992, the American Bar Association created the Commission on Nonlawyer Practice to examine the growing incidence of "nonlawyer practice" in the U.S. and to determine the implications of this practice on society and the legal profession. It defined "nonlawyers" as:

- Document preparers who fill out forms and court documents but provide no advice or representation

- Legal technicians who may fill out forms but typically provide advice or represent clients in areas such as family law, estate planning and probate, and bankruptcy
- Paralegals who work under the supervision of attorneys

After thirty-two months of public meetings and testimony from 400 witnesses, the ABA produced a summary report in 1994. It found that the entire form and scope of nonlawyer practice is expanding in response to an increased need by low- and moderate-income groups to seek solutions to their legal problems. It also found that nearly half of the state legislatures are considering proposals to authorize and regulate nonlawyer practice, including paralegals.

Six recommendations were made in the report, one of which concluded that the range of activities of traditional paralegals should be expanded, with lawyers remaining accountable for the paralegals' activities. While this was encouraging news for paralegals, the report has yet to be endorsed by the ABA Board of Governors nor have any of the six recommendations been acted upon. However, it is anticipated that most states will use the ABA report as the basis for deciding the future role of nonlawyer and paralegal activity in their state.

For example, in July 1996 Pennsylvania amended its UPL statute to increase the penalty for unauthorized practice of law to include paralegals. On the other hand, the Consumer Protection Committee of the Hawaii State Bar released a 1996 report stating "the Committee generally favors expanding the use of supervised legal assistance as a means of reducing costs for the public..." Today, thirty-four states are considering legislation governing nonlawyer activity.

Expanding paralegal roles. Recent challenges to UPL have come from paralegals who are involved in the profession's struggle to redefine itself and from citizen groups that want greater access to the legal system. Unauthorized practice laws affect paralegals by limiting the scope of their responsibilities and preventing them from offering services directly to the public. A relaxation of UPL would mean that paralegals could expand their roles and that new areas for employment would open up.

As the paralegal field matures, paralegals are performing more sophisticated tasks than ever before, specifically, tasks that were once performed by attorneys and might now be viewed as bordering on UPL. In addition, more paralegals than ever before are opening their own businesses, including legal form preparation services.

In terms of career planning, some paralegals consider these form preparation businesses to be a career advancement opportunity. Others consider them too restrictive and limited to be considered a step up. Many look at them as two distinct careers: paralegals working under the supervision of attorneys and those providing services directly to the public, called independent paralegals or legal technicians as defined by the ABA's 1994 Report on Nonlawyer Practice.

Paralegals are not the only ones challenging occupational laws. Faced with similar issues, nurses, midwives, podiatrists, and psychologists are among the medical paraprofessionals asking for the right to provide certain types of care currently restricted to physicians, such as giving examinations, prescribing medication, and performing certain types of surgery.

The physicians who are being challenged argue that their opposition to expanded paraprofessional responsibilities has more to do with a potential decrease in the quality of services than with an increase in competition. Some attorneys use the same argument against the challenges of nonlawyers.

On the flip side, most paraprofessionals don't consider themselves to be in competition with professionals who are educated and trained to perform complex services and procedures. They view themselves as providers of basic services at lower costs. I don't know many paralegals who would want to be responsible for a complicated legal transaction, but I know quite a few who could correctly prepare a simple incorporation at a much lower cost than an attorney.

There is no doubt that the UPL issue is a confusing one that becomes more complicated as time goes on.

ISSUE: REGULATION

The issue of regulation raises many questions. Are paralegals considered professionals? If so, shouldn't there be some sort of licensing procedure such as there is for other professions? What type of licensing is appropriate? What are the pros and cons of regulation? Will it expand or limit the paralegal profession? Who has the authority to regulate paralegals?

Who Should Be Regulated?

One of the most confusing aspects of this issue is trying to determine just who it is that should be regulated. Do full-time paralegals working under the supervision of attorneys need to be licensed? What about freelance paralegals working as independent contractors? And should nonlawyers, including independent paralegals who offer form preparation services directly to the public, be regulated?

For the purposes of this discussion, the term paralegal refers to the traditional paralegal working under the supervision of an attorney in a full-time, permanent capacity or as an independent contractor. The term legal technician, a phrase first used by the California State Bar in 1988, refers to a paralegal or other nonlawyer who offers legal services directly to the public and is not supervised by an attorney.

In March 1992, a symposium on paralegal regulation, sponsored by National Federation of Paralegal Associations (NFPA) was held in Houston, Texas. This was the first time such an event specifically focused on paralegal regulation. While there was disagreement among the registrants as to whether paralegals should be regulated, almost everyone agreed that there should be regulations on legal technicians.

What Type of Regulation Is Appropriate?

Unfortunately, those who do agree that licensing is necessary can't agree on what form it should take. Should it be voluntary or mandatory? Should there be continuing education requirements? Should the guidelines be formal or informal? Should there be enforceable contracts between the consumer and the nonlawyer? Should nonlawyers be required to register with various federal and state agencies? Should there be bar requirements? The list is endless.

The three types of regulation currently being considered by attorneys, paralegals, educators, and legislators include licensing, limited licensing, and registration.

- *Licensing* is the process by which an agency grants permission to persons meeting predetermined qualifications to engage in a given occupation or use a title. This is the most restrictive form of regulation.
- *Limited licensing* is the process by which a governmental entity grants authority to nonlawyers to assume roles customarily, but not exclusively, performed by lawyers. Its purpose is to expand the roles of experienced paralegals by allowing them to provide legal services to the public.
- *Registration* is the process by which individuals engaging in an occupation file specific personal information with an association or

agency. Usually, no educational or training requirements exist, and registration may either be voluntary or mandatory.

Arguments for Regulating Paralegals

As the paralegal field enters its fourth decade, there are still no barriers to entering the profession. The diversity of individuals working in the field, once a positive aspect of the career, is beginning to create its own problems. One such problem is the lack of standardization in terms of education, background, skills, and training. As we have seen in Chapter 5, there are many different types of educational options available, as well as other paths to a paralegal position. This lack of standardization is creating problems for employers hiring paralegals.

In addition, it is still unclear whether or not the paralegal field is a bona fide profession in the strictest sense of the definition. Paralegals are continually having to disprove the notion that they are not professionals because there are no set minimum standards such as education or examinations. Therefore, regulating paralegals would:

- Establish standards in terms of knowledge and skills that would help employers in hiring;

- Establish credibility for the profession and increase professional recognition;

- Expand paralegal roles if paralegals were licensed to perform functions that used to be done by attorneys; and

- Assist in providing affordable basic legal services to the public if a legal technician category of nonlawyers was authorized by state legislatures.

In 1986, the American Bar Association's Commission on Professionalism released a report recommending limited licensing of paralegals to perform basic legal services to the public. The commission stated:

> *It can no longer be claimed that lawyers have the exclusive possession of the esoteric knowledge required and are therefore the only ones able to advise clients on any matter concerning the law. Inroads on lawyer exclusivity have been made and will continue to be made. Lawyer resistance to such inroads for selfish reasons only brings discredit on the profession.*

In other words, the report encouraged direct nonlawyer competition with lawyers. This was an unprecedented move, since it was the first time the ABA proposed the concept of opening the legal services market to anyone other than lawyers.

One paralegal group that endorses regulation is the National Federation of Paralegal Associations. The issue of paralegal regulation was first discussed by the NFPA in 1988, when an ad hoc committee was formed to conduct preliminary research. Since then it has continued to refine and define its position on regulation. Today, the NFPA endorses a two-tiered approach to regulation. It believes that professional testing is a necessary step toward developing a regulatory program, and it has recently developed the Paralegal Advanced Competency Exam (PACE).

The NFPA does not believe that paralegals should be regulated by lawyers. According to the NFPA, regulation would benefit the paralegal profession by raising standards for training, addressing the need for greater consumer access to legal services, creating career paths for paralegals, and providing exemptions from UPL statutes.

Arguments Against Paralegal Regulation

Not all paralegals agree with the above rationale for regulating their profession. Some argue that the career is still too new to establish boundaries that might inhibit expansion of paralegal responsibilities. These individuals believe that the answer is not in regulation but in developing educational standards.

In addition, groups such as the National Association of Legal Assistants (NALA) believe that, since attorneys are ultimately responsible for paralegals' work product, consumers are protected, and, therefore, there is no need for paralegal regulation.

Other arguments against regulation include:

- It limits paralegal roles because it would specify what paralegals can and cannot do

- Paralegals do not serve the public, therefore licensing them is unnecessary

- Licensing paralegals would cut into attorney practice, since paralegals would be able to perform some basic services once done by an attorney

In conclusion, it appears likely that the regulation of paralegals will be decided on a state-by-state basis, further contributing to the already complicated issue of how to provide consumers with affordable legal services.

Regulating Legal Technicians

One solution to providing affordable legal services to all citizens would be to license and regulate nonlawyers to perform basic functions. The idea of nonlawyers has been around for over twenty-five years.

As mentioned in Chapter 1, in 1971 Ralph Warner and Nolo Press cofounder Charles Sherman established the WAVE Project, one of the first nonlawyer divorce form preparation services in the country. The project gave birth to the self-help law movement, the underlying principle of which is that, with some guidance and practical assistance, consumers can handle many legal matters on their own. It relies heavily on self-help law books and software for the preparation of wills, divorce papers, bankruptcies, and incorporations, among many other basic legal services, and the concept of independent paralegals to help consumers complete legal forms. In the past two decades, the WAVE Project has helped consumers save thousands of dollars in legal fees.

Perhaps the most common working example of the Nolo concept is the preparation of income tax forms. Citizens can opt to use a tax attorney, a CPA, or a tax specialist (such as H&R Block), or they can do their taxes themselves. In Nolo's view, this system can be applied to certain legal services such as divorce. A divorce is either uncontested (simple) or contested (involved). Depending on its complexity, the consumer would be able to choose from several types of services. (Under our current system, lawyers must be involved in even the simplest divorces.)

As the 1994 ABA Report on Nonlawyer Practice indicates, there has been a dramatic increase in nonlawyer practice nationwide, including individuals starting form preparation businesses.

In recent years, the task of regulating nonlawyers has been taken up mostly by state legislatures and state bar associations. California was one of the first states to recognize the need for a class of individuals other than lawyers who could offer legal services to the public. In 1987, the California Bar Association formed a special committee to look into the issue, but the idea was rejected by the board of governors in 1991. The California state legislature has since taken up the issue, and bills are now pending to license legal technicians. Legislation in other states, including New York, Texas, and Minnesota, have all been met with resistance, and no action has been taken.

In conclusion, it appears likely that the regulation of both paralegals and legal technicians will be decided on a state-by-state basis, further contributing to the already complicated issue of how to provide consumers with affordable legal services.

ISSUE: CERTIFICATION

Less controversial than the issue of unauthorized practice of law, but one that has been debated since the early 1970s, is the issue of paralegal certification. It's less controversial because the designation is voluntary and because there's less at stake for lawyers—after all, certification poses no threat to their livelihood.

By definition, certification is a voluntary form of regulation through which a nongovernment agency or association recognizes an individual who has met certain predetermined qualifications. Such qualifications include graduation from an accredited program, acceptable performance on qualifying examinations, and completion of a given amount of work experience.

Arguments for Certification

Proponents believe that certification provides standards for a specific level of paralegal proficiency, aids employers in the selection of prospective employees, and improves the status of the profession. They also believe that it helps to verify the completion of minimal education requirements and to reassure consumers of a paralegal's competence.

Among the major advocates of certification is the NALA. When it was incorporated in 1975, one of its top priorities was to develop standards for the field. After conducting a study, it developed the first and only national voluntary certified legal assistant (CLA) program in the country. The purpose of the CLA program, as mentioned in Chapter 6, is to establish a national standard of excellence and achievement, develop a means of identifying individuals who meet those standards, and bring professional recognition to the occupation by emphasizing that it is a learned profession. The CLA designation is also intended to deter people without the proper training and work experience from calling themselves legal assistants.

The program awards the CLA designation to paralegals only after they have met certain eligibility requirements and passed a qualifying exam. As of August 1996, more than 8,000 paralegals have received the designation. The NALA sees the designation as a mark of distinction and believes it has been established over the years as a means of recognizing paralegals who have met certain standards and attained a certain level of achievement.

Arguments Against Certification

Surprisingly, not all paralegals and lawyers agree about the benefits of certification. Some believe that, since certification is a voluntary designation, it does nothing to broaden the scope of paralegal responsibilities. The NFPA believes that certification does not address unauthorized practice of law issues and problems. In addition, the successful completion of a certification exam does not allow paralegals to offer legal services directly to the public. Furthermore, there is no evidence that certified paralegals earn more money or get better assignments than those without certification.

Through various forums, lawyers have also participated in the debate. In 1985, the ABA Standing Committee on Legal Assistants concluded that the benefits gained from certifying minimal paralegal competence don't outweigh the time, effort, and expense necessary to implement such programs. The committee found that any certification of advanced paralegal proficiency in specialized areas of law should be under the supervision of a board that includes lawyers, paralegals, educators, and members of the general public.

As long as certification remains voluntary, it will only represent a means of achieving professional recognition and status rather than a required standard for entry into the profession.

ISSUE: PARALEGAL EDUCATION

Should there be minimum educational requirements for all paralegals? Should there be standardized course requirements for all paralegal training programs as there are for all law schools? Should all paralegal training programs be ABA approved? Should all paralegals be required to have a bachelor's degree, a paralegal certificate, or both? If there are no standards in paralegal education or training, what criteria should employers use when hiring to ensure a standardized work product? Who should have the authority to decide the future of paralegal education and training: paralegals, attorneys, paralegal educators, or all three? These are just some of the questions being asked about paralegal education today.

It has been suggested by professionals outside of the legal industry that education, not regulation (in the form of licensing or certification), is the key to professionalism within most occupations. But for the paralegal profession, this is easier said than done.

The quality of paralegal education is an ongoing concern of paralegals, educators, attorneys, and employers. As mentioned in Chapter 5, unlike professions that adhere to strict educational standards, the paralegal field is still open to individuals with a wide variety of backgrounds. In addition, paralegal education can range from three-month certificate programs to four-year bachelor's degree programs and everything in between. At this time the only standard in paralegal education is whether or not a program is ABA approved.

The ABA Standing Committee on Legal Assistants believes that the best means of increasing the proficiency and quality of paralegals is to increase the number of ABA-approved training programs and the number of continuing education programs.

Both the NFPA and the NALA appear to be in agreement when it comes to the issue of paralegal education. Both associations work directly with the ABA approval commission. But while everyone involved seems to agree that educational standards for paralegals need to be developed, guidelines have yet to be adopted industrywide.

Some progress has been made on that front. In an event called The Conclave, which first took place in March 1988, representatives from various paralegal, attorney, and educational associations met to discuss, among other things, paralegal education. In the report that resulted from that event, all groups agreed that:

- There is a substantial amount of diversity in the types of paralegal training offered and in the educational backgrounds of students

- There are difficulties in teaching because of the lack of standardized textbooks and methods of instruction

- The information available to employers regarding the quality of paralegal training programs that would enable them to make informed hiring decisions is insufficient

- There is a trend toward hiring entry-level paralegals with bachelor's degrees

- The general education requirements within paralegal training programs serve to eliminate the disparity between the diverse educational backgrounds of students

- The minimum of 15 hours of legal specialty courses currently required by the ABA guidelines is too low

- A campaign to educate attorneys on high-quality paralegal education should be instituted by the ABA, state and local bar associations, and paralegal associations

Some of the other significant recommendations made in this report focused on changes in curriculum design. The report stated that a minimum of 30 units of general education be required and should include courses in computers, math or accounting, history, government, and communication. Such courses should focus on analytical and quantitative skills. In addition, the report recommended that factual and legal research, legal ethics, the American legal system, and the professional legal environment be included in legal specialty course requirements. The report also emphasized that internships should be a part of every paralegal training program.

The recommendations of The Conclave represent a step toward the development of standards in paralegal education, but perhaps most significant is the communication that the meeting fostered between the various groups.

Not much has changed in the past decade; there's still no standard way of entering the profession. As you learned in Chapter 5, there are still a variety of paralegal programs and a number of degrees that one can obtain in order to become a paralegal. A lot depends on the law of supply and demand in a particular area of the country.

NFPA's current position is that while it recognizes that a two-year degree with an emphasis in paralegal studies is enough for some markets, future paralegals should have a four-year degree.

Without a standard for paralegal education and training, chances are good that state legislatures will begin to look at the issue more closely, just as they are doing with paralegal regulation and legal technicians. In the future, paralegal education may be decided in state legislatures. While the issue of paralegal education is far from being resolved, it's safe to assume that education requirements are likely to become more rigorous.

ISSUE: EXEMPT OR NONEXEMPT?

Should paralegals be compensated for overtime? According to current U.S. Department of Labor rulings, paralegals are covered under the wage and hour provisions of the Fair Labor Standards Act of 1938 (FLSA) and are considered nonexempt employees who must receive overtime pay after 40 hours of work in one week. This has created quite a stir.

What is the problem? Under the FLSA, exempt employees are those who are employed in bona fide executive, administrative, or professional capacities; exercise a large degree of independent judgment in their jobs; and are relatively free of supervision by others. The labor department believes that problems related to unauthorized practice of law statutes make it impossible for paralegals to meet the independent judgment qualification of exempt employees. The implication of this interpretation is that, in terms of employment law, the paralegal field may not even qualify as a profession.

Paralegals are divided on this issue. Some believe that the exempt classification would enhance their professional status. Others feel that it would give employers a legal way of having them work long hours without being paid overtime. Still others believe that there's nothing demeaning or less professional about nonexempt status.

Since the paralegal profession is rapidly changing, it's possible that future studies of the profession by the U.S. Department of Labor will recommend that it be given an exempt status. However, an April 15, 1995 U.S. Department of Labor opinion letter (prompted by an employer who sought to determine whether a particular paralegal was exempt or nonexempt) found that the paralegal was a nonexempt employee and was therefore entitled to overtime pay.

While this opinion does not appear to bode well for a profession that is attempting to define and promote its professional status with employers, only 41 percent of paralegals responding to *Legal Assistant Today* magazine's 1996 salary survey were considered nonexempt employees by their employers.

ISSUE: UNDERUTILIZATION OF PARALEGALS BY ATTORNEYS

Since the inception of the paralegal profession several decades ago, great strides have been made in the quality, complexity, and level of paralegal assignments and responsibilities. Paralegals have been around long enough now for most enlightened employers to have a pretty good idea of what they can do. There are still exceptions to this, though, and some paralegals still find themselves frustrated and underutilized.

The type of work delegated to a paralegal depends on the attorney, size of firm, type of practice, and qualifications of the paralegal. In 1994, *Legal Assistant Today* conducted an interesting study on the factors that influence an attorney's decision about whether or not to delegate challenging work to paralegals. The survey was sent to over 25,000 attorneys in the state of Michigan. Forty-six percent of the respondents used paralegls, while 54 percent did not. Of the 54 percent who did not, 41 percent said their secretaries did the work. These results indicated either a lack of understanding of what a paralegal does or, if given an economic choice, the preference of a secretary over a paralegal.

Interestingly, the study concluded that it is the paralegals who are not taking enough initiative in getting better quality work when they are dissatisfied with the level of work they are doing. While 89 percent of those that used paralegals claimed that they have expanded their parale-gals' job responsibilities, only 8.3 percent said their paralegals asked for these expanded roles.

This survey points out the need for paralegals, particularly those who are entering the profession, to be aware of the fact that they must be proactive in seeking out better assignments in order to take control of their careers. If this survey is any indication, most attorneys will respond favorably to expanded paralegal assignments, provided the paralegal has proved that he or she is capable of handling increased duties.

MIXED SIGNALS

The paralegal profession is reaching a critical point in its evolution. While some bar associations and legislatures are looking to expand paralegal roles through the licensing of legal technicians, others are seeking to limit them.

A Step Backward

A single mom in Syracuse, New York, in a financial jam decided to file for personal bankruptcy by hiring an independent paralegal to file the Chapter 7 documents. She paid just $269 for the filing as opposed to $750, which is what a lawyer would have charged. Unfortunately, in response to a series of complaints from the U.S. Trustee's Office in

Albany, New York, a federal bankruptcy judge ruled that the independent paralegal could charge no more than $100 for the bankruptcy filing.

Another independent paralegal was told by a bankruptcy judge in Georgia that she could no longer use legal software designed specifically to generate bankruptcy documents to help her customers.

These are just two examples of how the legal system is preventing the expansion of paralegal roles.

One of the best illustrations of a reversal in attitude toward the paralegal profession came in November 1990, when the New Jersey State Supreme Court's Committee on the Unauthorized Practice of Law concluded in Advisory Opinion No. 24 that freelance paralegals working as independent contractors are not adequately supervised by attorneys and that these paralegals are functioning outside the supervision of attorneys and are therefore engaged in UPL. The court believed that freelance paralegals are so removed from attorneys that there is little opportunity for direct supervision. The ruling required that employers hire paralegals as employees, not independent contractors.

The ruling not only threatened the livelihood of many freelance paralegals, it also affected many law firms that used freelance paralegals. Many people wondered what the difference was between using a freelance paralegal and a freelance or temporary secretary.

In response to the ruling, lawyers representing freelance paralegals in New Jersey asked that the Supreme Court reverse the UPL Committee's opinion. In May 1992, after several months of hearings and debate, the Supreme Court did just that; it reversed Opinion No. 24, stating that the evidence does not support a ban on freelance paralegals.

As a former freelance paralegal myself, it surprised me that the courts were making such a fuss over freelancing. In reading part of the Supreme Court's decision, I found it interesting to note that the court admitted that no satisfactory, all-inclusive definition of what constitutes the practice of law has ever been devised. If the courts can't even come up with an adequate test of what constitutes practicing law, paralegals have a long road ahead of them when it comes to the UPL issue.

Some Encouraging Signs

Despite this setback, the profession is making headway in terms of increased recognition and expanding roles.

Independent paralegals and legal technicians. As was mentioned earlier, proposals to allow nonlawyers, including paralegals, to provide limited legal services directly to the public are being examined by several states. The fact that the ABA decided to do a study on this issue at all and has concluded that there is a need for nonlawyer practice, is perhaps the best indication that the paralegal profession is moving forward.

Representation before administrative boards. Can paralegals working in law firms appear before administrative courts and represent their firm's clients?

The question has been brewing in California for some time and is closely related to the UPL issue. In February 1989, the California State Bar Association issued an opinion that permits paralegals who work in law firms to represent their firm's clients before administrative courts. The bar's Standing Committee on Professional Responsibility and Conduct found that adequately supervised paralegals can appear before the Workers' Compensation Appeals Board to file petitions and motions as long as the client consents to the use of a paralegal.

The ABA's 1994 study on nonlawyer practice found that there are thirty-eight federal and numerous state administrative agencies that permit representation by nonlawyers in areas such as unemployment compensation, social security, immigration, worker's compensation, public health, and employment discrimination, to name a few.

Furthermore, the U.S. Supreme Court has determined that the Administrative Procedure Act, which permits federal administrative agencies to use nonlawyers to represent parties in their proceedings, pre-empts any state UPL laws.

The ability of nonlawyers, specifically paralegals, to represent individuals in agency proceedings is an important step in expanding paralegal roles. While it is a far cry from deregulation, it signals a loosening of UPL and the expansion of paralegal responsibilities. As you can see, the unauthorized practice of law issue affects more than just paralegals.

ABA associate membership. In 1987, the ABA voted to amend its bylaws to create an associate status for paralegals, which allows them to participate in many ABA activities. The ABA believes this will further its efforts to ensure that the public receives effective, affordable legal services. The ABA encourages all paralegals to take advantage of associate status in order to enhance their working relationships with attorneys. While this is by no means an earth-shattering development, it does signal an effort toward greater communication between paralegals and attorneys.

Malpractice insurance. "A malpractice suit against a legal assistant is inevitable," said H. Jeffrey Valentine, the National Paralegal Association (NPA) executive director, in the December 2, 1988, edition of the *New York Times*. "It will send shock waves through the entire paralegal community, but the independents will have the most to fear."

Knowing that malpractice suits are in the future, the NPA is planning to offer malpractice insurance to paralegals. The National Federation of Paralegal Associations (NFPA) already has such a program in place called the Paralegal/Legal Assistant Professional Liability Insurance Program. It is available through the NFPA Risk Purchasing Group, P.O. Box 6104, Chicago, Illinois 60680, or call 800-989-NFPA.

The availability of such insurance further illustrates the growing status of the profession.

Martindale-Hubbell listings. In 1992, for the first time in its history, the *Martindale-Hubbell Law Directory* allowed law firms to include biographical information on nonlawyer support personnel, including paralegals. The amount and type of information is at the discretion of the employer. Paralegal associations believe that the inclusion of paralegals provides important recognition for the profession as a whole as well as for the individual paralegals listed.

Clearly, all the issues mentioned in this chapter will continue to be debated for some time—particularly the issue of licensing nonlawyers and paralegals. But the future looks bright for this profession. I am hopeful that one day we will realize our two most important goals: the ability to provide people with greater access to affordable legal services and the expansion of paralegal roles and responsibilities in many of these services.

Afterword:
The Future for Paralegals

Minds are like parachutes—they only function when open.
Thomas Dewar

■

The fallout from the recession of the early 1990s is behind us. The economy is growing, inflation is in check, and the stock market is at an all-time high. For those entering the paralegal profession in the late 1990s, the outlook couldn't be brighter. As consumers continue to demand affordable legal services, paralegals will play a greater role in alleviating the burden of high fees. Just what that role will be, however, is still being debated by paralegals, bar associations, and state legislatures.

Will paralegals continue to work for attorneys—or will they evolve into professionals with the ability to offer basic legal services directly to the public? If they do the latter, will their authorization to practice law involve licensing or certification, or will formal paralegal education and training be enough? Does our legal system have room for two levels of professionals, or will it continue to be dominated by lawyers?

One thing is certain: paralegals represent change, and change is almost always met with resistance, particularly from those who benefit from the status quo. It is this sense of change—being part of a profession that's still evolving, still striving to overcome resistance, and still trying to define itself—that I find one of the most interesting aspects of the occupation.

Future Trends

For those who become paralegals in the late 1990s, their career will be exciting and challenging. The challenges come from a more complex legal environment in which lawyers are being forced to examine their profession in new ways. Increased competition for clients, specialization, greater use of technology and computers, the advent of advertising and marketing, and the emergence of alternative dispute resolution methods have transformed the entire legal industry and have affected the responsibilities of paralegals. And the changes will continue into the next decade. Though predicting the future is risky, I believe, as many industry watchers do, that the following trends are emerging:

189

- **Education:** Greater emphasis is being placed on education. More employers are requiring a bachelor's degree or a paralegal certificate, or both. With an increasing pool of available paralegal graduates, it will be more difficult to enter the field without a formal paralegal education.

- **Competition:** Competition for paralegal jobs will increase dramatically as more individuals discover the field. Although the U.S. Department of Labor estimates that over 70,000 paralegal jobs will be created by the year 2005, to be competitive, those entering the field will be required to have more knowledge, skills, and training than their predecessors.

- **Work environments:** Given the downsizing of large firms in the early 1990s, the trend will be to hire more paralegals in small- to medium-size firms. In addition, as corporate law departments handle more work in-house instead of using costly outside counsel, there will be greater opportunities for paralegals in corporations.

- **Technology:** Technology will continue to dramatically change the way lawyers practice law and will open up new opportunities for computer-literate paralegals. And the level of computer expertise required by employers will increase.

- **Job responsibilities:** Paralegals are performing more sophisticated and substantive legal work than ever before. This has led to greater job satisfaction and the trend toward choosing the paralegal profession as a long-term career rather than merely as a stopgap measure or a stepping stone to other work.

- **Specialties:** Paralegals will have greater opportunities to become experts in particular legal areas as the practice of law becomes more specialized. This will result in greater job satisfaction and increased compensation.

- **Contract work:** The trend toward hiring temporary and independent contractors is increasing in most areas of business, and law firms are no different. Firms will continue to use temporary paralegals and attorneys to fill in the gaps.

- **Advancement opportunities:** More nonlegal employers will realize that paralegal skills and knowledge can be useful in their areas of business. Paralegals will have more choices when it comes to applying their experience to law- and nonlaw-related areas.

- **Paralegal businesses:** More paralegals will start their own businesses, as either freelancers or independent paralegals. This will occur as a result of corporate downsizing and the desire among many paralegals for a more flexible work environment.

- **Public recognition:** Recognition of the paralegal profession by the general public will continue to increase. Clients and consumers of legal services will become more aware of the benefits of using paralegals to reduce legal fees. As a result, the career will continue to gain in popularity.

- **Older workforce:** Because of continuing changes in the job market, the paralegal profession will become a second career choice for many individuals in their forties and fifties. As a result, we'll see a trend toward older paralegals entering the field.

- **Issues:** Paralegal regulation and education will continue to be hotly debated issues. Since paralegals can't agree on a solution themselves, it's unlikely that these issues will be settled in the near future. Licensing paralegals or other nonlawyers to perform basic services to the public will mostly likely be decided by state legislatures and not bar associations. Since this idea is extremely controversial, it will probably be some time before paralegals will view this as a career option.

A Final Word

As the paralegal profession matures, the lines between attorney and paralegal will blur even more, and the inevitable conflict between the old and the new will continue. Such conflict was predicted in another context by Alvin Toffler two decades ago in *The Third Wave*.

In his bestselling book, futurist Toffler examined the major waves of change that affect social, economic, and cultural systems worldwide. The First Wave of change was the agricultural revolution. It was overtaken by the Second Wave—the industrial revolution. Toffler predicts that the Third Wave, the postindustrial era that we are now in, will sweep aside many of the changes introduced in the Second Wave. Toffler writes, "the unevadable fact remains that the Third Wave production in the office, as it collides with the old Second Wave systems, will produce anxiety and conflict as well as reorganization, restructuring, and—for some—rebirth into new careers and opportunities."

I believe the paralegal profession fits in well with Toffler's prediction. Change is opportunity. And many opportunities lie ahead for paralegals.

APPENDIXES

Appendix A: Paralegal Associations

National Association of Legal Assistants, Inc. (NALA)
1516 S. Boston, #200
Tulsa, Oklahoma 74119
918-587-6828 / 918-582-6772 (fax)
Web site: www.nala.org

Membership in the NALA is open to individual paralegals and paralegal associations. The NALA publishes a bimonthly newsletter called *Facts and Findings* and offers the only certified legal assistant designation in the country. Contact the NALA for a list of member paralegal associations in your area.

National Black American Paralegal Association
P.O. Box 28024
Washington, D.C. 20038-8024
202-452-7485 / 202-371-0416 (fax)

Formed in 1994, the organization seeks to "cultivate, promote, and recognize black paralegal professionals." The NBAPA will offer seminars, a newsletter, and a job bank.

National Federation of Paralegal Associations, Inc. (NFPA)
P.O. Box 33108
Kansas City, Missouri 64114-0108
816-941-4000 / 816-941-2725 (fax)
Web site: www.paralegals.org

The NFPA is composed of over fifty state and local independent paralegal associations. It publishes a quarterly newsletter called the *National Paralegal Reporter*. If your local paralegal association is a member of the NFPA, you automatically receive the *National Paralegal Reporter* when you join your local association. Contact the NFPA for a list of member paralegal associations in your area.

Appendix B: Other Helpful Associations

American Association for Paralegal Education (AAfPE)
P.O. Box 40244
Overland Park, Kansas 66204
913-381-4458 / 913-381-9308 (fax)

The AAfPE serves paralegal educators and administrators of institutions that offer paralegal training programs. The AAfPE publishes the *Journal of Paralegal Education* once a year.

American Bar Association (ABA)
Standing Committee on Legal Assistants
750 North Lake Shore Drive
Chicago, Illinois 60611
312-988-5000 / 312-988-6281(fax)
Web site: www.abanet.org

Paralegals can join the ABA as associate members. The association publishes *Legal Assistants Update* annually, which contains articles on the paralegal profession written by paralegals and attorneys. The ABA also offers other publications relevant to the paralegal profession.

Association of Legal Administrators (ALA)
175 East Hawthorne Parkway, Suite 325
Vernon Hills, Illinois 60061
847-816-1212 / 847-816-1213 (fax)

The ALA's purpose is to enhance the competence and professionalism of the legal administrator and the legal management team. The ALA publishes the journal *Legal Administrator*.

Legal Assistant Management Association (LAMA)
638 Prospect Avenue
Hartford, Connecticut 06105-4250
860-586-7507 / 860-586-7550 (fax)
Web site: www.lamanet.org

The association disseminates information regarding legal assistant management and promotes the professional standing of legal assistant managers.

Appendix C: Suggested Reading

Facts & Findings
1516 S. Boston, #200
Tulsa, Oklahoma 74119
918-587-6828 / 918-582-6772 (fax)

This is the official publication of the National Association of Legal Assistants. Published quarterly with two issues in the first quarter. Subscription rate for nonmembers is $25 for four issues.

Legal Assistant Today
P.O. Box 25202
Santa Ana, California 92799-9900
714-755-5450 / 714-751-2709 (fax)

For students and entry-level and experienced paralegals alike, this is the bible of the paralegal profession. Published by James Publishing Inc., subscriptions are $52.98 per year.

National Paralegal Reporter
P.O. Box 33108
Kansas City, Missouri 64114-0108
816-941-4000 / 816-941-2725 (fax)

Published quarterly by the National Federation of Paralegal Associations, Inc. Subscriptions are $25 per year.

Appendix D: Paralegal Recruiters

The following is a list of employment agencies nationwide that specialize in both permanent and temporary paralegal placement. The list is by no means complete. Since addresses and phone numbers can change at any time, contact your local paralegal association for up-to-date information on recruiters in your area.

Federal Reports Inc.
1010 Vermont Ave., NW, Suite 408
Washington, D.C. 20005
202-393-3311 / 202-393-1553 (fax)
Web site: www.attorneyjobs.com

Publishes the book *The Paralegal's Guide to U.S. Government Jobs: How to Land a Job in 140 Law-Related Careers.*

Interim Legal Personnel
2000 West Commercial Blvd., Suite 132
Fort Lauderdale, Florida 33309
800-249-9474 / 305-938-7770 (fax)

Landmark Legal Professionals
2055 Gateway Place, Suite 400
San Jose, California 95110
408-451-3911 / 408-451-3921 (fax)

Lawstaf Inc.
One Atlantic Center
1201 W. Peachtree St., Suite 4830
Atlanta, Georgia 30309
404-872-6672 / 404-892-3180 (fax)

Olsten Staffing Services
175 Broad Hollow Rd.
Melville, New York 11747
800-WORK NOW
Web site: www.olsten.com

Pathways Personnel, Inc.
120 Montgomery Street, Suite 320
San Francisco, California 94104
415-391-2060 / 415-391-6118 (fax)

Special Counsel, Inc.
800-737-3436
Web site: www.specialcounsel.com

Offices in Atlanta, Baltimore, Boston, Cleveland, Jacksonville, Los Angeles, New
York, San Francisco, and Washington, D.C.

Templeton & Associates
15 South 5th Street, Suite 1000
Minneapolis, Minnesota 55402
612-332-8079 / 612-332-6690 (fax)

The Wallace Registry
Gothic Park
43 Woodland Street
Hartford, Connecticut 06105
800-248-4LAW
(National Headquarters)

Appendix E: Paralegal Salaries

There are several factors that influence paralegal salaries, including type
of employer, years of experience, legal specialty area, and geographical
region. The following figures taken from a national survey conducted in
1996 by *Legal Assistant Today* represent base salary as a function of these
factors and serve only as a guideline. They do not include bonuses,
overtime, or other forms of compensation. Also, since the figures reflect

1996 salaries, you'll need to adjust them by adding approximately 6 percent per year (the average annual salary increase for paralegals for the past two years) to estimate salary levels for subsequent years.

Salary Survey Findings

	Average
National	$ 32,415

By Employer

Law firm	31,933
Corporation	36,158
Government Agency	28,289

By Years of Experience

1–5 years	28,570
5–10	32,659
10–15	38,198
15–20	41,131
Over 20	39,379

By Region*

Eastern region	31,426
Central region	30,166
Midwestern region	32,960
Western region	38,543

*Eastern region = Connecticut, Delaware, Florida, Georgia, Maine, Maryland, Massachusetts, New Hampshire, New Jersey, New York, North Carolina, Pennsylvania, Rhode Island, South Carolina, Vermont, Virginia, Washington, D.C., West Virginia.

Central region = Alabama, Arkansas, Illinois, Indiana, Iowa, Kentucky, Louisiana, Michigan, Minnesota, Mississippi, Missouri, Ohio, Tennessee, Wisconsin.

Midwestern region = Arizona, Colorado, Idaho, Kansas, Montana, Nebraska, New Mexico, North Dakota, Oklahoma, South Dakota, Texas, Utah, Wyoming.

Western region = Alaska, California, Hawaii, Nevada, Oregon, Washington.

Source: Copyright © 1997 James Publishing, Inc. Reprinted courtesy of *Legal Assistant Today* magazine. For subscription information, call (800) 394-2626.

As mentioned in Chapter 7, another excellent source of paralegal salary information is from The National Federation of Paralegal Association, Inc. It conducts a comprehensive paralegal salary survey every two years. The latest one will be available at the end of 1997.

Appendix F: Paralegal Training Programs

There are a number of sources available to locate paralegal programs in your area. One of the most accurate would be your local paralegal association. Another resource that is continually being updated is the Web site for the National Federation of Paralegal Associations (NFPA) at www.paralegals.org. The site lists the names, addresses, and telephone numbers by state for over 800 programs in three categories:

- Non-ABA-approved programs
- ABA-approved programs
- AAfP- member programs

Programs are marked with an "A" for programs approved by the American Bar Association, an "E" for members of the American Association for Paralegal Education (AAfPE), or an "AE" for both.

Keep in mind that, as mentioned in Chapter 5, non-ABA-approval does not necessarily mean that the program being offered is not of good quality and reputable.

The American Bar Association also publishes a list of ABA-approved paralegal programs. You can purchase a copy of the ABA's "Guide for Legal Assistant Education Programs" for $7.50 by contacting the American Bar Association's Service Center at 312-988-5522.

Reader note: Prior to 1994, the ABA made this list available to the public for free (this list was reprinted in the second edition of this book). Since 1994, the ABA has charged for the list and doesn't give reprint permission, which is why the list is not reprinted here. Also, the NFPA does not give permission to reprint any part of the list of paralegal programs from its Web site.

Bibliography

Adams, Susan. "The Guild Fights Back." *Forbes*, November 18, 1996.

American Bar Association. "Guidelines for the Approval of Legal Assistant Programs." Chicago: American Bar Association, 1973.

American Bar Association Commission on Nonlawyer Practice. "Nonlawyer Practice in the United States: Summary of the Factual Record Before the Commission." Chicago: American Bar Association, 1994.

American Bar Association Commission on Professionalism. "... In the Spirit of Public Service: A Blueprint for the Rekindling of Lawyer Professionalism." Chicago: American Bar Association, 1986.

American Bar Association Section of Economics of Law Practice and the Standing Committee on Legal Assistants. *Working with Legal Assistants: A Team Approach for Lawyers and Legal Assistants*, vols. 1 and 2. Edited by Paul G. Ulrich and Robert S. Mucklestone. Chicago: American Bar Association, 1980-81.

American Bar Association Special Committee on Legal Assistants. "The Paraprofessional in Medicine, Dentistry, and Architecture." Chicago: American Bar Association, 1971.

———. "The Training and Use of Legal Assistants: A Status Report." Chicago: American Bar Association, 1974.

American Bar Foundation. "Supplement to the Lawyer Statistical Report: The U.S. Legal Profession in 1985." Chicago: American Bar Foundation, 1986.

Baber, Brad. "The Other Side of the Mountain." *Legal Assistant Today*, November/December 1996.

Blackman, Josh and Andrew Z. Adkins II. "Lawyers Embrace The Internet." *Law Products*, January/February 1997.

Bogen, Deborah. "New Specialist Trend Brings Big Rewards." *Legal Assistant Today*, January/February 1996.

Bowdren, Brian L. " 'Storyselling': Laser Disc in the Courtroom." *At Issue*, July 1991 and August 1991.

Brookes, Diane, Cheryl Evans, Richard Leiter, and Brent Roper. "The Best Legal Software for Paralegals." *Legal Assistant Today*, May/June 1996.

"California State Bar Crushes Attempt to Legalize Some Legal Technician Services." *Legal Assistant Today*, January/February 1992.

Caudron, Shari. "Overtime Pay: Overrated or Making Ends Meet?" *Legal Assistant Today*, January/February 1996.

Cazares, Leanne C. "First PACE Exams Given." *Legal Assistant Today*, September/October 1996.

Cohen, Alan. "The AmLaw Tech Survey." *AmLaw Tech*, Fall 1986.

Cohn, Steve. "New Hampshire Bar Governors Take Strides for Paralegal Education." *Legal Assistant Today*, March/April 1992.

Colorado Bar Association. "CBA Legal Assistants Committee Proposed Guidelines for the Utilization of Legal Assistants." *Colorado Lawyer*, 15 (February 1986).

Covington, Betsy. "Managing Legal Costs, Services." *American City & County*, January 1995

Crank, Kim, and Kim Marshall, "Superfund and the Legal Assistant." *Michigan Bar Journal*, November 1991.

Cuneo, Alice, Michele Galen, and David Greising. "Guilty: Too Many Lawyers and Too Much Litigation." *Business Week*, April 13, 1992.

Curriden, Mark. "Law Firms in the 21st Century." *Legal Assistant Today*, September/October 1995.

Dunn, Karen L. "In Search of Plain English." *Facts & Findings* 14, no. 4, January 1989.

Edwards, Ivana. "Simple and Inexpensive Litigation Support on Your PC." *Legal Assistant Today*, March/April 1992.

Estrin, Chere. "The Manager's Perspective." *Legal Assistant Today*, July/August 1996.

Fellers, James D. "State of the Legal Profession." *American Bar Association Journal* 61, September 1975.

Granat, Richard S., and Deborah M. Knight. "A Computer Training Program for Paralegals." *Legal Economics* 14, March 1988.

Hall, Michael J. "Bar Rejects Legal Technician Issue." *Sonoma County Daily Herald-Recorder*, September 5, 1991.

Handbook on Paralegal Utilization. California Alliance of Paralegal Associations, Copyright 1992, 1993, 1995.

Harrington, Linda. "Freelancing for Fun and Profit." *National Paralegal Reporter*, Fall 1983.

Helmich, Nancy L., and Roger A. Larson. "Legal Assistants in Public Law: Their Role in Attorney General Offices." *Legal Assistants Update*, vol. 5. Chicago: American Bar Association, 1986.

Hines, Lyla O. "The National Federation of Paralegal Associations: An Association of Associations." *National Paralegal Reporter*, Fall 1988.

Honigsburg, Peter J. *Cluing into Legal Research: A Simple Guide to Finding the Law*. Berkeley: Golden Rain Press, 1979.

"How to Choose a Paralegal Education Program." Web site www.para-legals.org: National Federation of Paralegal Associations, Inc.

Hunt, Stacey, CLA. "Trading Places: Is The Grass Really Greener In The Small/Large Firm?" *Legal Assistant Today*, March/April 1996.

———. CLA. "Paralegals Deemed Production Workers." *Legal Assistant Today*, July/August 1996.

Jacobs, Gordon L. "Legal Technology: Present and Future Trends." *Legal Economics*, November/December 1987.

Jacobstein, J. Myron, and Roy M. Mersky. *Legal Research Illustrated*. Mineola, N.Y.: The Foundation Press, Inc., 1977.

Johnson, Beverlee. "Legal Administrator Grows Up." *Legal Administrator*, Summer 1986.

Jones, James W. "The Challenge of Change: Practice of Law in the Year 2000." *Vanderbilt Law Review* 41, no. 4, May 1988.

Kaiser, Susan A. "Regulation: A New Forecast on a Timeworn Question." *National Paralegal Reporter*, Winter 1990.

Kamicar, Sheryl. "The Paralegal's Role in Foreclosures." *National Paralegal Reporter*, Fall 1991.

Keefe, Kathleen. "State Bar OKs Appearance by Paralegals." *At Issue*, March 1989.

Klein, Janet (producer), and John Stossel (correspondent). "Are They Worth the Price You Pay?" Transcript from *20/20*, July 28, 1989.

Kording, Niccol, and Leanne Cazares. "For Love or Money." *Legal Assistant Today*, January/February 1997.

Larson, Roger A. "Certification of Legal Assistants: A Report on an American Bar Association Survey." *Legal Assistants Update*, vol. 5. Chicago: American Bar Association, 1986.

"Lawyers Make a Case for It." *Information Week*, August 24, 1992.

"Lawyers on Lawyers in America." 1994 Research Report, Global Research, a division of Euromoney Publications, PLC. *Wall Street Journal*, May 13, 1994.

"Lean Times Hit Legal Profession." *San Francisco Chronicle*, March 9, 1992.

"Legal Assistant Information Sheet." American Bar Association, 1991.

"Licensure and Its Effects on Paralegal Practice." *National Paralegal Reporter*, Winter 1991.

Littleton, Arthur D. "ABA Position Paper on Licensure or Certification, and Definition of Legal Assistants." *Legal Assistants Update*, vol. 5. Chicago: American Bar Association, 1986.

Mattson, Eric. "Legal Scholars Urged to Keep Writing Simple." *Facts & Findings*, 15, no. 4, January 1989.

Miller, Jolene. "Regulation: Responding to the Crisis in the Delivery of Legal Services." *National Paralegal Reporter*, Winter 1991.

Miró, Angela B. "Ten Thousand Documents and Counting." *Legal Assistant Today*, March/April 1996.

Morrow, Rebecca. "Paralegals–Nine; Attorneys–One." *Legal Assistant Today*, March/April 1996.

Muir, David W. "Technology in the Courtroom: Computer Animation." *At Issue*, May 1991.

Myers, Michelle, and Kumar Raman. "Sweet-Talking Clients and Intransigent Bureaucrats: Immigration Paralegals Know Them All." *National Paralegal Reporter*, Winter 1991.

Neher, Kathleen, Howard D. Schwager, and Michelle T. Fecik. "Why Aren't More Attorneys Using Paralegals?" *Legal Assistant Today*, January/February 1996.

"Net Know-How a Career Booster?" Paralegals Online column, *Legal Assistant Today*, September/October 1996.

"1995 *Paralegal Compensation and Benefits Report.*" National Federation of Paralegal Associations, Inc, 1995.

"Non-Lawyer Personnel in 1992 *Martindale-Hubbell Law Directory*." *At Issue*, July 1991.

Paralegal Responsibilities. Deerfield, Ill.: National Federation of Paralegal Associations, 1996.

The Paralegal's Guide to U.S. Government Jobs: How to Land a Job in 140 Law-Related Careers. 7th ed. Washington, D.C.: Federal Reports, Inc., 1996.

"Paralegal Status Sign: Malpractice Insurance." *New York Times*, December 2, 1988.

Petropulos, Diane. "AAfPE Conference Highlights." *Legal Assistant Today*, January/February 1992.

———. "Certification Exams in Your Future?" *Legal Assistant Today*, January/February 1996.

———. "Computer Training Resources." *Legal Assistant Today*, May/June 1996.

Polsinelli, Joanne. "Future Paralegal Roles." *National Paralegal Reporter*, Fall 1988.

"President Nixon Approves Legislation Creating a National Legal Services Corporation." *American Bar Association Journal* 60, September 1974.

"Report of the Conclave." *National Paralegal Reporter*, Spring 1988.

Roper, Brent D. "11 Ways Computers Can Make You More Efficient." *Legal Assistant Today*, May/June 1992.

Ruse, Peggy, and Joe Whelan. "Results of the NFPA Survey of Non-Traditional Paralegal Responsibilities." *At Issue*, January 1990.

Safran, Verna. "The Boom in Going Bust: Opportunities for Paralegals in Bankruptcy Law." *Legal Assistant Today*, May/June 1992.

Schaberg, Robert E. When, Why and How You Should Use a Litigation Support Data Base. 1988. Unpublished paper.

Shimko-Herman, Deanna. "Regulation Proposals Find National Audience." *National Paralegal Reporter*, Winter 1991.

Silas, Faye A. "Is Paralegal Certification Worthwhile?" *Bar Leader*, July/August 1986.

Simonsen, Craig. "Litigation Skills Spill Over into Environmental Law." *National Paralegal Reporter*, Spring 1991.

Stern, Gary. "Mandatory Licensing: A Step Forward or Backward?" *Legal Assistant Today*, March/April 1997.

Syllabus prepared for the convenience of the reader by the Office of the Clerk of the New Jersey Supreme Court In Re Opinion No. 24 of the Committee on the Unauthorized Practice of Law.

"Texas to Offer Legal Assistant Specialty Exams." *Legal Assistant Today*, September/October 1992.

"The Future of Law Office Computing... ." *Law Office Computing*, February/March 1997

U.S. Bureau of Census. "Current Business Reports." 1988 Service Annual Survey. Washington, D.C.: 1989.

———. 1987 Census of Service Industries. Washington, D.C.: 1989.

———. *Statistical Abstract of the United States 1985*. 105th ed. Washington, D.C.: 1985.

———. *Statistical Abstract of the United States 1987*. 107th ed. Washington, D.C.: 1987.

———. *Statistical Abstract of the United States 1989*. 109th ed. Washington, D.C.: 1989.

———. *Statistical Abstract of the United States 1991*. 111th ed. Washington, D.C.: 1991.

———. *Statistical Abstract of the United States 1996*. 116th ed. Washington, D.C. 1996.

Webb, Wendi. "1st Annual 'Best Firms to Work For' Awards," *Legal Assistant Today*, March/April 1996.

———. "Riding the Technology Wave." *Legal Assistant Today*, September/October 1996.

———. "The New Age of Electronic Discovery." *Legal Assistant Today*, May/June 1996.

———. "The Paralegal Job Market: Going Strong!" *Legal Assistant Today*, July/August 1996.

Wertheim, Lynda F. "Career Paths for Legal Assistants." *Legal Assistants Update*, vol. 4. Chicago: American Bar Association, 1984.

"What's Hot." *Information Week*, May 12, 1997.

Whiteside, Frances. "Paralegal's Reach A Consensus." *Legal Assistant Today*, July/August 1992.

Work, Clemens P. "A New Challenge to Doctors and Lawyers." *U.S. News & World Report*, August 23, 1984.

"Wrangles with the Feds May Get Easier to Resolve." *Wall Street Journal*, April 8, 1991.

Zimmermann, Kim Ann. "Lawyers Break Ties to Paper." *Imaging Magazine*, August 1992.

About the Author

After graduating from the University of Hartford in 1974 with a bachelor's degree in psychology, Barbara Bernardo spent the next five years pursuing a career in dance and theater. She began working as a paralegal in 1979 while continuing her interests in the performing arts.

Ms. Bernardo has over thirteen years of experience as a paralegal and legal administrator in law firms and corporations in San Francisco, New York City, and Hartford. She has worked in a wide variety of practice areas, including securities, corporate law, real estate, litigation, antitrust, mergers and acquisitions, environmental law, and employee benefits.

Ms. Bernardo received a Master of Business Administration degree and currently works as a marketing manager for Lawgic Publishing Company, a legal software company. She resides in Sonoma County, California, with her husband, David.

INDEX